SPRING FEVER GOBBLER

Michael Hanback

Published by

 **krause
publications**

700 E. State Street • Iola, WI 54990-0001
Telephone: 715/445-2214

Please call or write for our free catalog of outdoor publications.
Our toll-free number to place an order or obtain a free catalog is 800-258-0929
or please use our regular business telephone 715-445-2214 for
editorial comment and further information.

Library of Congress Catalog Number: 95-82122
ISBN: 0-87341-423-3
Printed in the United States of America

Dedication

To my dad, Will Hanback, who introduced me to this wonderful obsession so many springs ago.

Contents

Acknowledgments

I am deeply indebted to everyone who helped turn this book from a dream to a reality.

To Cecil Carder, Jim Clay, Jim Conley, Jim Crumley, Mark Drury, Tom Duvall, Toxey Haas, David Hale, Ron Jolly, Chuck Jones, Bill Jordan, Harold Knight, Will Primos, Ronnie "Cuz" Strickland and many other fine people too numerous to mention in the turkey hunting industry. Thanks for all the glorious days we have shared together in spring gobbler country. Your respect for God's great outdoors—not to mention your expertise in hunting and calling our magnificent quarry—has rubbed off on me in myriad ways to become vital parts of this book. I hope you know how much I value your friendship and support.

I wish to thank Gerry Bethge, Jim Casada, Tom Fulgham, and all the other outdoor magazine editors who have seen fit to publish my turkey hunting articles over the years. A special debt of gratitude goes to everyone at Krause Publications for believing in me and *Spring Gobbler Fever*.

Last but certainly not least, I owe a heartfelt thank you to my wife, Pat, and young sons Clay and Emery. You put up with me as I rattle around the house and bolt out the door at 4:00 a.m. on April mornings here in Virginia. You stand by me as I venture off to turkey hunt in many faraway places each spring. Your love, patience and support mean more to me than you can ever imagine. Without you, this book would never have been possible.

Introduction

We can all rejoice in the amazing comeback of the American wild turkey.

In the early 1900s, the grand game bird teetered precariously on the brink of extinction. Today, less than a century later, more than 4 million wild turkeys roam more square miles of habitat than any other game bird in North America. Due to healthier-than-ever turkey populations, spring gobbler hunting seasons occur in all the United States except Alaska, and in several Canadian provinces as well.

Every current and potential turkey hunter owes a debt of gratitude to state and federal wildlife agencies and the National Wild Turkey Federation. Funded largely by hunters' dollars, these organizations have initiated successful trap-and-transplant programs that have restored wild turkeys to all corners of their ancestral range, and introduced the adaptable birds into new habitats across the country.

I envision good things on the horizon for our quarry. The three most abundant subspecies of turkeys—the Eastern, Rio Grande and Merriam's—should continue to expand their populations and ranges well into the future. Thanks to solid management programs in its dwindling Florida habitat, the Osceola strain should hold its own.

America's soaring number of wild turkeys has created (and will continue to foster) unprecedented opportunities for a burgeoning number of spring turkey hunters. According to a recent gun-industry survey, as many as 5 million gobbler chasers may hit the greening woods this season. Turkey hunting is one of the fastest growing shooting sports on the planet!

To that end, the timing of this book, which I have strived to make the definitive text on spring gobbler hunting, could not be better.

The primary objective here is to help you call in and shoot more long-bearded gobblers with razor-sharp spurs. Whether you are a novice, intermediate or seasoned turkey hunter, I trust you will find within these pages a multitude of fresh and innovative scouting, gear, setup, calling and shooting strategies that will enable you to score consistently.

As you read this book, keep one important point in mind. Turkey hunting is a different game today than it was 30, 20 or even 10 years ago. In many regions, record numbers of hens and subordinate toms encircle boss gobblers during most phases of the wild turkey's spring mating season. With so much competition out there from live turkeys (not to mention other hunters), you need specialized strategies.

Many of the following chapters deal heavily with hunting and calling dominant gobblers who travel in "breeding flocks," something you will likely encounter this spring and in seasons to come. This tactical advice, which has never before appeared in book form, will help you fill your turkey tags.

While this text is highly instructional, it is not all about how to kill wild turkeys. My second goal here is to convey the true essence of spring gobbler hunting—the roller coaster of thrills, frustrations and high-wire tension that is challenging long-bearded monarchs on misty mornings and sun-glistening afternoons.

I have weaved throughout these pages some memorable gobbler encounters, focusing on all sorts of things that have happened to me during the past 25 springs of serious turkey hunting across the United States. From successful hunts to blown opportunities to spectacular misses, I have attempted to paint a picture of what it is like to duel America's craftiest and most unpredictable game bird, whom I hunt with the utmost admiration and respect. After reading this book, I hope you will pursue our magnificent quarry with the same frame of mind.

Here's to long beards, sharp spurs and many safe and memorable days in spring gobbler country.

Michael Hanback
Summer, 1994

The Eastern is the most abundant and widespread wild turkey in North America. It is also the most difficult subspecies to hunt. Hone your calling skills on crafty Eastern longbeards, and you'll be primed to duel the three remaining races of gobblers. (Photo by Leonard Lee Rue III)

Chapter 1

The Quarry

Four major subspecies of wild turkeys inhabit North America. Habitat-related idiosyncrasies aside, a gobbler is a gobbler wherever he is found—beautiful, sharp-eyed, jittery, vocal and uncannily unpredictable.

This is a tactical hunting book, not an ecological treatise on America's grandest game bird. Still, the pursuit of spring gobblers is like any other form of hunting. To be successful, you must know your quarry.

We begin this chapter with an overview of the four similar yet wonderfully distinct strains of wild turkeys that roam across 49 states (no turkeys in Alaska) and several Canadian provinces. We then examine the traits, vocalizations and behavioral patterns of gobblers during the spring mating season. This data lays a firm foundation for the refined hunting and calling strategies that are the core of this book.

The Eastern Wild Turkey

The Eastern subspecies, *Meleagris gallopavo silvestris,* is the most abundant and widespread wild turkey in North America. An estimated 2.6 million to 3 million birds inhabit 37 Eastern, Southern and Midwestern states. The subspecies has been successfully transplanted in California, Oregon and Washington. Eastern-strain turkeys are expanding their range north into Ontario.

Easterns live in diverse habitats, from Southern swamps to Northeastern mountains to Midwestern farmlands. Hardwood-and-pine forests interspersed with fields and waterways provide prime turkey habitat.

In the spring, a mature Eastern gobbler stands over three feet tall and weighs 17 to 21 pounds. Heavier strains of Eastern birds are common, especially in Missouri, Iowa and other Midwestern and Northern states.

A tom's black-tipped breast feathers reflect a bronze sheen in sunlight. His tail, comprised of 18 long rectrices that he spreads out into a magnificent fan when strutting, is chestnut brown and black with brown or dark-buff tips.

In springtime, a year-old gobbler, or jake, has a three- to four-inch beard and round nubs for leg spurs. A two-year-old tom typically has a seven- to nine-inch beard and spurs that measure 1/2 to 7/8 of an inch. An Eastern male three years of age or older has a beard that exceeds 10 inches and one-inch or longer spurs. A few mature gobblers have two or even three beards.

As is the case with all subspecies of wild turkeys, Eastern hens are noticeably smaller than toms. Hens weigh 8 to 11 pounds and are dusky-brown in color.

A gobbler three years of age or older, the kind you should be hunting for, has a beard that exceeds 10 inches in length. His spurs are sharp, hooked and more than an inch long.

A mature Osceola tom may weigh only 16 or 17 pounds in the spring. But the Florida swamp dweller has a long, thin beard and razor-sharp spurs. (Photo by Lovett Williams)

The Eastern is universally regarded as the most difficult subspecies of turkey to dupe with a calling device. The primary reason is that in many regions today, the crafty gobblers travel with harems of hens during most phases of the spring breeding season. Heavy hunting pressure can also cause longbeards to become "call shy," a dilemma discussed later in this book.

The Osceola Subspecies

The Osceola wild turkey, *Meleagris gallopavo osceola,* is the namesake of the famous Seminole Indian chief who led his tribe in a bloody border war against the Americans in the early 1800s. Today, 75,000 to 100,000 Osceola birds roam pine woods, oak hammocks, cypress swamps and cattle pastures in central and southern Florida.

The Osceola is the smallest and most streamlined of the four turkey subspecies. A mature gobbler in peak breeding mode may weigh only 16 or 17 pounds. The Osceola's coloration is similar to the Eastern's, although a Florida tom's onyx breast and back feathers reflect more iridescent reds, greens and blues in sunlight. An Osceola tom's primary wing feathers, predominantly black with narrow white veins, are distinctive.

The beard of a dominant Osceola drags the ground, but is generally thinner than an Eastern's. The Florida turkey has long legs for wading in swamp water. His long, curved and razor-sharp spurs are prized by sportsmen.

A secretive and sporadically gobbling turkey that roosts in cypress swamps, the Osceola ranks second only to the Eastern as the most challenging subspecies to hunt in the spring.

The Merriam's Turkey

The Merriam's strain, *Meleagris gallopavo merriami,* inhabits 15 Western states from South Dakota to Idaho to New Mexico. The subspecies can also be found in pockets of suitable habitat in the lower portions of Alberta and Manitoba.

An estimated 200,000 Merriam's roam western plains, prairies and mountains. The densest concentrations of turkeys are often found in the scrub-oak and ponderosa-pine foothills of the Rockies. Merriam's flocks are loosely migratory, inhabiting snow-capped peaks in summer and moving to lower elevations in winter.

In size, the Merriam's turkey is comparable to the Eastern. A gobbler's silky tail coverts and fan tips are distinctive, colored tan to white and shining like polished ivory in the bright western sunshine.

The westernmost wild turkey is also our most beautiful quarry. The Merriam's tail coverts and fan tips shine like polished ivory in the sunshine. (Photo by Leonard Rue Enterprises / Irene Vandermolen)

His black breast feathers reflect lavender, red and bronze. The Merriam's is generally regarded as the most beautiful wild turkey on earth. The tips of a mature gobbler's beard and spurs are often sanded off by the dry, rocky terrain he inhabits, giving our westernmost turkey even more character.

In the Rockies, chasing free-roaming Merriam's in the spring is a lot like hunting autumn elk. You must often climb and descend miles of ridges and canyons, glassing with binoculars, maneuvering around and calling extensively in hopes of intercepting a gobbler and his hens as they travel between preferred feeding, watering, strutting and roosting areas.

The Rio Grande Subspecies

In range and appearance, the Rio Grande turkey falls between the Eastern and the Merriam's subspecies, hence its scientific classification *Meleagris gallopavo intermedia*. The Rio is native to the south-central plains and is most abundant in that region today. The subspecies has been successfully stocked in several West Coast states.

While nearly 700,000 Rios inhabit 13 states, the subspecies is often called the "Texas wild turkey" for good reason. A whopping 85 percent of America's Rio Grande population roams the Lone Star State.

Rios love open habitats—typically scrub oak and mesquite prairies with tree-lined streams for roosting. In western Kansas and Oklahoma, the birds feed and strut in grainfields.

I find the Rio to be the heavyweight of the wild turkey clan. A mature, copper-colored tom with long, pink legs may weigh 22 to 25 pounds or more in springtime. Like Merriam's, Rios often have rubbed beards and spurs.

There is a nasty rumor floating around that the Rio Grande is a piece of cake to hunt. Let me put things in perspective. Run across a plains gobbler who travels solo in the spring, and he'll normally work nicely to a call. But a long-bearded Rio who travels with a harem of hens can be every bit as finicky and unpredictable to call as a notoriously tough Eastern or Osceola.

Turkey Traits

The wild turkey's eyesight is legendary. He sees much more crisply than a man with 20/20 vision. Most amazing to me is a gobbler's uncanny ability to pick up even the slightest movement, whereupon he ducks his head and is gone in a flash.

Rio Grandes inhabit open, broken country in the south-central plains. Contrary to popular opinion, a mature Rio gobbler traveling with hens can be as difficult to call as a wily Eastern tom. (Photo by Leonard Lee Rue III)

A turkey's eyes are set in the sides of his head, which gives him monocular vision. But he more than makes up for this lack of three-dimensional sight by cocking his head left or right to determine the distance to potentially dangerous flashes in the brush. A turkey can twist his periscopic neck 360 degrees, which in effect gives him eyes in the back of his head.

Most biologists agree that wild turkeys can assimilate color. For example, both hens and subordinate gobblers react to the changing reds, blues and whites of a dominant tom's head during the mating ritual. A gobbler's color-pulsing head helps to stimulate hens into breeding, and sends a signal to suppressed toms to keep their distance.

You must respect the turkey's keen eyesight—but not to the point where you become frozen and scared to death to shift your shotgun or bow as a gobbler struts to your calls. Complete camouflage and smooth, well-timed moves (covered in detail in subsequent chapters) are keys to getting the drop on incoming toms.

Even though wild turkeys do not have ear lobes or flaps to funnel in sound waves, they have excellent hearing. Keep this in mind as you hunt. Brush slapping against clothes or the metallic click of a shotgun safety being depressed can send a gobbler ducking for cover.

Wild turkeys have a poor sense of smell, so you do not have to play the wind as when deer hunting. There is an old saying among spring gobbler hunters: "If a turkey could smell, you'd never kill one!" I think that is about right.

I am forever amazed by the quickness and agility of a 20-pound gobbler. Upon encountering danger, he prefers to run and does so like a spooked rabbit. A turkey ducks his head, tucks low to the ground and darts away through the ground foliage before you can begin to shoulder your shotgun.

A gobbler's strong, muscular legs (the drumsticks are tough eating!) not only allow him to run like a track star, they catapult the turkey into the sky as if he were shot from a cannon. Heavy-winged gobblers are strong fliers for 200 to 400 yards—flight speeds in excess of 50 miles per hour have been recorded. After short bursts of flight, turkeys set their wings and glide, often for a mile or more to elude danger.

As if the gobbler's keen senses and agility were not enough to keep you spinning in circles, you must understand that this is one jittery bird you are fixing to hunt. I have chased 15 species of big game across North America over the past two decades. I have yet to encounter a more instinctively spooky and unpredictable creature than the wild turkey.

Gobblers are skittish the moment they peck from their eggshells. They become extremely wary over the years as they adapt to their habitat and elude foxes, bobcats, coyotes and a host of other predators, including you and me.

Just how jittery is the wild turkey? Many times I have watched gobblers suddenly break strut, hop five feet right or left and then stand in one place for five minutes to burn holes in the brush with their keen eyes. Sometimes it was the shadow of a flying crow that spooked the turkey. Other times it was the sound of a rotten tree limb falling. In many cases, the spooky turkey was just being a spooky turkey!

Another old turkey hunting adage goes like this: "The only thing predictable about a gobbler is that he is apt to do something unpredictable." Respect your quarry's keen senses, evasive maneuvers and survival instincts. And remember to expect the unexpected when you venture into the spring woods.

The Calls Of Spring

All four strains of American wild turkeys have the same vocabulary, which consists of more than two dozen calls, each carrying a unique message. Any dialectical differences in turkey talk can be traced to the acoustics of each subspecies' habitat. For example, a

The wild turkey's loud, attacking gobble is nature's ultimate mating call. You feel a gobble as much as you hear it. Toms gobble in the spring primarily to attract hens, but also to exude their dominance over subordinate males. (Photo courtesy Perfection Turkey Calls)

forest-dwelling Eastern tom seems to rattle the dense foliage with his gobbling. But on the open Texas plains, a Rio Grande's gobbling sounds more subtle and clear-throated.

Here are the primary calls that hens and gobblers use to communicate throughout the spring courtship ritual. Most of the vocalizations you will mimic on a variety of calling devices, as covered in-depth in subsequent chapters. The last two vocalizations you will not use to lure turkeys, but learning to recognize and decipher them is paramount in hunting situations.

Yelp: Both hens and gobblers yelp in rhythmic, four-to-10-note series to locate other turkeys throughout the day. Longer and shorter yelping sequences are common. Two-note hen yelps—*kee-awk, keeawk*—run the gamut from high-pitched to raspy. Gobbler yelping is slower in cadence and often more deep-throated than hen calling.

Tree Yelp: A soft, short version of the standard yelp, turkeys of both sexes tree call as they stir on their limbs each morning, saying to other birds in the area, "All's well over here."

Cluck: Gobblers and hens utter single, soft-to-loud staccato notes to locate and communicate with other turkeys.

Cutt: Lonely or lost hens use fast, irregular series of clucks when searching for other turkeys. Cutts last five to 15 seconds and are typically loud and aggressive.

Cackle: Hens cackle in 10- to 20-note series when pitching up to or down from their roosts, and also when flying across water, canyons, etc. Cackles, which are comprised of fast, irregular clucks and yelps, are followed up with more subtle clucks as the turkeys hit the ground and gather themselves after flight.

Purr: This soft, fluttering call is uttered by both hens and gobblers as they feed along. When relaxed and close together, turkeys purr to communicate contentment.

Gobble: Toms gobble primarily to attract hens, but also to exude their dominance over subordinate males. Gobbles typically last one to two seconds—the initial loud, attacking notes are the easiest to hear from afar. I find that toms can control the intensity of their gobbling; for instance, they can roar to attract distant hens and gobble softer when ladies are in sight.

Mature toms are well-versed in gobbling, but jakes in their first spring are just learning the mating call. Young gobblers try their best to roar, but often end up tossing out a weird-sounding mix of gobbles and squawky yelps. Ah, but don't be fooled. I've called to turkeys bellowing like the king of the woods, only to have a jake with a four-inch beard show up proudly in hopes of breeding his first hen.

Strutting gobblers in peak breeding mode drum to attract hens. Keying in to the soft, two-note melody allows you to keep tabs on longbeards as they work to your calls. (Photo by Leonard Lee Rue III)

Aggravated Purr: Gobblers emit loud, aggressive fighting purrs and rattles as they posture to battle for the right to breed hens.

Drumming: Once thought to be the soft humming of a strutting gobbler's shimmying tail feathers, biologists now agree that drumming is a melodious, two-note *pfftt,duuummm* vocalization forced deep from a gobbler's chest. A tom drums for the same reason he gobbles — to attract hens.

A gobbler can control his drumming as he varies his gobbling, drumming love tunes either softly or intensely depending on the proximity of hens. Depending on its intensity and the terrain and foliage in an area, drumming can be heard 60 to more than 100 yards away on calm spring days.

While you will not mimic a gobbler's drumming, you need to key in to the two-note melody. It will allow you to locate non-gobbling but drumming toms on their spring roosts. More importantly, zeroing in on drumming enables you to keep close tabs on a gobbler as he struts into your calling.

Putt: Hens and gobblers emit loud, sharp alarm putts when they sense danger. This is obviously not a call you want to hear in a hunting situation, but again one that you must focus on. Staring down your shotgun barrel at a gobbler who suddenly putts, you must fire immediately if you have a clean-killing shot. The turkey has seen you or sensed trouble and is fixing to duck his head and run.

The spring pursuit revolves around the wild turkey's three-phase breeding season. Stage two, when mature gobblers are surrounded by harems of hens, is the most difficult time to call in a longbeard. (Photo courtesy Perfection Turkey Calls)

The Spring Courtship Ritual

The spring pursuit revolves around the wild turkey's frenzied breeding season, which kicks off in February in southern climates and extends into May in northern regions. The mating time can be broken down into three phases, each of which finds gobblers exhibiting unique behavior.

The urge to breed is triggered by the increasing hours of daylight in late winter and early spring, which stimulates the sex hormones of gobblers. Unusually cold, rainy weather can delay the onset of turkey mating. Conversely, warm weather can speed up the courtship ritual.

Some breeding occurs while turkeys are still in winter flocks, especially when warm weather dictates an early spring. During late winter and early spring, turkeys are congregated in three types of flocks—mature and young hens, jakes and mature gobblers.

Within each flock, hens and gobblers establish rigid pecking orders. Early breeding is almost always done by dominant gobblers who hook up with the first receptive hens of spring.

As the days become longer and warmer, the primary breeding season fast approaches. Hens begin to break up into small flocks and disperse widely into nesting areas. Dominant gobblers in the social hierarchies follow the hens and begin driving some subdominant longbeards and jakes from their breeding zones.

Years ago, alpha gobblers had little trouble running off a limited number of subordinate toms. But with record numbers of wild turkeys per square mile in many regions today, many old gobblers are forced to let subordinate toms, often their siblings, travel with them throughout the spring. The dominant birds still rule the roost. The suppressed longbeards can tag along, but they are allowed to breed few hens, unless they can steal away for a few minutes each day to have some fun. I call this the "fringe gobbler" phenomenon (see Chapter 11).

As alpha toms suppress subdominant males, they begin gobbling like crazy to attract harems of hens. Gobblers, extremely polygamous, are the ultimate male chauvinists. They bring down the woods with lusty gobbling as they try to round up as many hot little hens as possible.

Hen-gathering time, which may last several days or a week, represents the first of two gobbling peaks. In years of normal weather, this gobbling crescendo typically occurs from mid-March to early April in southern regions, and in mid- or late April in northern and western states.

Once dominant toms corral harems of hens, gobbling activity, as a whole, decreases dramatically. At dawn, most turkeys gobble one or two times on the roost, though a few cocky birds roar frequently and with lust. Most all dominant gobblers then fly down with their ladies and clam up. The toms may gobble a few times or not at all later in the day as they strut around and breed hens. This phase is the dreaded "gobbling lull." Chapter 10 is devoted to the difficult task of calling silent and henned-up toms.

Impregnated hens soon begin slipping off to lay one egg each day, usually in late morning or early afternoon. Hens prefer to nest at the bases of trees or around fallen logs with dense cover. It takes nearly two weeks for hens to lay full clutches of 10 to 12 eggs. Hence, you are faced with a couple of weeks of sporadic gobbling.

Having filled their nests, the hens desert the gobblers to incubate their eggs. Still ready and willing to breed, dominant gobblers prowl for new hens, and the second gobbling peak often explodes.

Notice I say "often." With more hens than ever inhabiting many regions today, dominant gobblers do not have to venture very far or gobble too lustily to attract fresh ladies. In fact, many toms simply strut around and pick up new hens as the old ones leave to incubate their eggs. In this scenario, the gobblers smile all over themselves as they rotate between hens! Thus, the second gobbling peak may last only a few days or be nonexistent in your hunting area.

Timing Is Everything

It is paramount to understand the phases of the wild turkey's breeding season as they occur in your hunt zone. The pursuit of spring gobblers, you see, is a lot like hunting white-tailed deer in the fall. In both sports, timing is everything.

The most predictable time to deer hunt is during the pre-rut, when hot bucks prowl for does on the brink of estrus. The optimum time to chase turkeys is in early spring, when fired-up toms travel widely and gobble with zest to attract hens.

When bucks chase and breed does during the peak rut, the hunting becomes highly unpredictable. When gobblers strut and tread hens during the second phase of spring, the calling is downright tough.

The first few days of the whitetail post-rut, when bucks search for leftover does to breed, is a hot time to hunt. Turkey calling can be excellent late in the spring, when mature gobblers attract the last receptive hens of spring.

Your calling success will soar if you time your hunts to coincide with peak gobbling phases. Toxey Haas of Mossy Oak camouflage (right) and I hit it just right in Alabama several springs ago.

Many serious deer hunters, myself included, schedule vacation days for the last week of the pre-rut and/or the first week of the post-rut, when bucks are most patternable and fewer hunters are in the woods. You should adopt a similar strategy when planning your spring turkey hunts.

If you are in the enviable position of hunting every morning during spring gobbler season (many turkey addicts I know somehow make the time to go each day), no problem. But if like most of us your vacation time is limited, try to hunt as many days as possible during the first gobbling peak. In the frenzy of gathering their harems, gobblers will often trip over their beards running to your hen calls.

Trouble is, many states do not open spring seasons until after the hen-gathering phase normally occurs. Wildlife officials theorize that this allows gobblers to breed a maximum number of hens before they are possibly harvested by hunters. This seems to be sound policy, and I have no problem with it.

But some states, especially in the South, schedule spring seasons that overlap the initial gobbling peak. Opening week is often a prime time to hunt. The gobblers are hot and have not been called to for months (possibly even a year in regions where no fall turkey seasons occur). However, opening week is also when most hunters take off work. You will run into a lot of calling competition, especially on public lands.

While the first week of any season is apt to offer fair to good hunting, it is not necessarily the optimum time to fill your turkey tags. During an unusually warm spring, gobblers may have gathered their hens early. When opening day rolls around, the gobbling lull may be on in earnest. Conversely, cold weather may delay hen-gathering for a week or so. In either case, you might be better off scheduling your hunting time for the second or even third week of the season.

This is a tough call, so how do you make it? For starters, contact a state upland bird biologist to determine when gobblers typically gather hens in your region. Then, beginning in February, monitor the weather. If it appears peak gobbling will fall during opening week, have at it. But if you think cold weather will push hen gathering back a week or so, tell your boss you will play hooky the second week of the season. You will hear more gobbling and bump into fewer hunters.

In states where short seasons occur late in the spring, the gobbling lull often coincides with opening week (again, weather can be a variable, so monitor it closely). In this case, I would definitely plan to hunt later in the season. A second gobbling peak may or may not occur in your area. But as hens begin to incubate their eggs, the odds of finding a solo tom soar in your favor.

Just how important is timing your spring gobbler hunts? Try this one on for size.

One year, two buddies and I traveled to Alabama the first week of April. The gobbling was hot and we killed 10 longbeards. A classic hunt!

The next spring, we returned to the same area the first week of April. It had been an unusually warm winter and spring was weeks ahead of schedule—the gobblers were henned-up tight and had severe cases of lockjaw. We worked our tails off to shoot three toms over seven days of intense calling.

Due to spring season dates, vacation time, family commitments, fickle weather and a host of other factors, timing your hunts to coincide with peak gobbling phases is difficult and often impossible. Hunt when you can—a poor day in the spring turkey woods beats a good day at work anytime—but try to go when gobblers are gathering hens or between their ladies. You will hear more gobbler music, have more fun and double your odds of success.

The serious hunter should use only top-quality gear. When going to war with spring gobblers, I carry everything I need in my turkey vest and leave super-fluous items at home.

Chapter 2

Serious Turkey Gear

We turkey hunters are gear fanatics. Camouflage, locator calls, diaphragms, slates, boxes, shotguns, lovads, decoys, wings, blinds and on and on.

Actually, toying with today's dazzling array of gobbler-chasing stuff is one of the most enjoyable facets of the spring obsession. But with a zillion turkey products on the market and more rolling off the assembly lines every day, you must be careful not to overdose.

Wade right in amongst all the camouflage, calls, firepower and accessories. Then begin to pare things down and assemble a modus operandi. Carry everything you need for going to war with spring gobblers, but leave any superfluous items behind. This way, you hunt at peak efficiency.

Here, we focus on the secondary but vital gear that lays the groundwork for a serious and streamlined turkey hunting system. Calling devices and shotguns and loads, the flashy centerpieces of the spring pursuit, are examined in-depth in the next two chapters.

Camouflage

Gobbler hunters are addicted to camouflage, and for good reason. Developing a hat-to-boot concealment system is a prerequisite to luring the keen-eyed quarry within shotgun or bow range.

Fifteen years ago, a handful of clothing companies offered a couple of military camouflages to break your outline in the woods. Today, more than 20 manufacturers are using photo images, computer graphics, improved textile technology and a lot of human ingenuity to produce an array of camo patterns designed to turn you invisible in every imaginable turkey terrain.

Regardless of where you hunt, you cannot go wrong by selecting a quality "bark" camouflage like Mossy Oak, Realtree or Trebark. Available in many pattern designs and color schemes, these prints feature swirls of overlaid green "leaves" and gray, brown and black

Today's excellent "bark" camouflages create a 3-D effect that hides you from the sharp but monocular eyes of gobblers. Choosing a camo pattern that you like and trust gives you an edge in the turkey woods.

"limbs." This three-dimensional effect is what hides you from the probing but monocular eyes of gobblers.

Cloaked in Mossy Oak, I have hunted all four subspecies of American wild turkeys. I have also fooled my share of crafty toms while decked out in Realtree and Trebark. I have high regard for all these patterns and recommend them without reservation. I trust them to turn you and me invisible whether we set up to call in a Florida swamp, the New Mexico high country or any habitat in between.

Trusting your camouflage is an intangible that can give you an edge in the turkey woods. It allows you to sit tight when a wily tom struts in close—you know he will not spot your outline in the cover. Faith in your camo also allows you to move when you must—either to ease your shotgun barrel onto a gobbler's neck, or to back away from a hung-up turkey before circling around to a more strategic calling spot.

Regardless of which brand of camouflage you choose, try interchanging various multi-colored patterns to refine your concealment plan. I do not believe this is vital to success, but it is an intriguing idea nonetheless.

"It's easy to take concealment to a higher level by mixing and matching your camo," my friend Toxey Haas, mastermind of the Mossy Oak patterns, told me on a spring turkey hunt years ago. "For instance, wearing our Full Foliage shirt (with prominent green leaves) and Fall Foliage pants (lots of autumn-colored leaves) is unbelievably effective for spring gobbler hunting."

I contemplated this awhile, then decided Haas' theory made a lot of sense. So I decided to try it. On many hunts across the country, I've worn green-leafed shirts to blend with the blossoming spring foliage, and brown-pattern pants to match the rotting leaves and duff of the forest floor.

My findings? The mix-and-match concept further helps to break your outline and gives you even more confidence that a gobbler will not bust you with his sharp eyes.

Choose loose-fitting camouflage pants, shirts and jackets that allow you to hunt comfortably on warm to hot spring days. And select your camo to fool not only the legendary eyes but also the keen ears of your quarry.

Go with lightweight cotton camo on warm days, and chamois or a modern synthetic like Worsterlon for cool-weather hunts in Eastern or Merriam's range. These soft materials brush quietly against limbs when you approach a gobbling turkey. They make no unnatural swishing noises that might alert a skittish bird of your desire to sneak into calling range and rob him of his beard and spurs.

Masks & Gloves

Many hunters spend a lot of time and money choosing camouflage pants, shirts and jackets, then pluck from the shelf the first face mask and gloves they see. This can be a terrible mistake! Face and hand shields are not merely turkey hunting tokens. Neglect a practical design, and it can cost you a gobbler.

Don't let a little detail cost you a tom! Choose a comfortable face mask that allows 180 degrees of peripheral vision. For concealment and safety, camouflage gloves should thoroughly cover your wrists.

Years ago, I wore a tight-fitting head net with eye holes the size of quarters. One glorious April morning, I worked an old tom for close to an hour before he finally clammed up. I knew nerve time was upon me—the turkey was either coming or had tired of my game and was drifting away from my setup.

Twenty minutes later, having seen no feathers and heard no gobbling or drumming, I decided to relocate in hopes of striking the gobbler again. As I pushed up from my tree, an alarm putt rang like a school bell in my ears. The turkey had slipped in silently to my left, in a blind spot created by that faulty face mask! I ripped it off my head and watched in horror as the huge longbeard ducked through the foliage, catapulted skyward and sailed away through the sunlit oaks.

Never again. I stuffed that damned mask into a stump, where I hope it rotted a slow and lingering death.

Most camouflage designers and game call companies have wised up, and now offer all sorts of face masks and head nets that provide both ample concealment and peripheral vision. One of my favorites is Primos' Half Mask, which you wear around your neck when prospecting for turkeys, then pull up over your nose when you set up to do battle. This leaves a couple of inches of open space between your mask and cap, allowing you to easily cut your eyes left and right in search of an incoming tom.

I sometimes wear a three-quarter mask or full head net for maximum concealment. If you prefer this style, check out Perfection's Bandit, M.A.D.'s Chameleon or Quaker Boy's Bandito. All models are comfortable and have large eye slots or rings for maximum visibility.

It is relatively easy to reach up under a half-mask and slip a diaphragm call into your mouth. But this can be a worrisome inconvenience when wearing a three-quarter mask or head net. More distressingly, tugging at a head net and reaching up under it to change mouth calls creates movement you do not need when a gobbler is working in close. If your head net does not feature a mouth slot, cut one in it to simplify the use of diaphragm calls. I always do.

A couple of thoughts on choosing and using camouflage gloves. The popular cotton models have a tendency to bunch down around your wrists after heavy use. What do you think a beaming ray of sunlight off your watch face would look like to an approaching gobbler? Also, an exposed piece of arm moving in the cover could be mistaken for a gobbler's white head by a reckless nitwit who might sneak in as you work a gobbling turkey.

Clipping the fingertips from your gloves allows you to easily dig calls and other little stuff from your vest in the heat of a gobbler duel. You may find that you control a slate call better with exposed fingers.

Many turkey call companies sell camo gloves with tight- fitting, five-inch uppers to alleviate such problems. Incorporate these into your system.

I normally clip away the thumb and forefinger tips of my gloves for a couple of reasons. First, this allows me to easily find my shotgun's safety and trigger when a big gobbler suddenly pops into view. Also, exposed fingers make it easy to dig into your vest for diaphragm calls, box-call chalk and other little stuff in the midst of a gobbler duel.

Spartan-Realtree makes camouflage gloves with pre-cut thumb and forefinger slits. I love them! You don't have to cut up your gloves to get the dexterity you need. Consider adding a pair of these to your turkey hunting system.

Turkey Vests

A well-designed, camouflage turkey vest is the heart of your concealment and hunting system. All the little stuff that you must carry into the woods for gobbler battles can be organized in this functional piece of equipment.

The best turkey vests on the market have a dazzling amount of pocket space, which you should designate for each piece of gear. For example, choose a small top pocket for your diaphragm call case. Locator calls go in the left bottom pocket; slate calls and pegs find a home in the lower right one. A box call is secured in a specially designed and zippered compartment. Compact binocular, flashlight and other little items are stowed in inner pockets.

The key is to condition yourself to keep every piece of gear in its designated slot on every turkey hunt. Then when you instinctively reach into your vest for a diaphragm, box or slate with a turkey firing back gobbles 60 yards away, you know the call will be at your fingertips where it is supposed to be.

There are many excellent Mossy Oak, Realtree and Trebark vests on the market today. Choose one that is roomy enough to fit comfortably over a chamois jacket on cool mornings. But be sure the vest is not too big because its nylon straps will fall off your shoulders when you wear only a thin, long-sleeve T-shirt on hot days. This is annoying.

A good vest will have an ample rear pouch for carrying rolled-up rain gear and other large items—and hopefully for packing out an 18-pound longbeard from time to time! Most modern vests have flip-out Blaze Orange flaps on the back. These offer excellent safety insurance when toting birds from heavily hunted areas.

Choose a vest with a flip-down seat cushion that snaps securely to the back (most new vests feature thin, foam seats). Back in my younger and more macho days, I thought cushions were for wimps. Now I cannot imagine waiting out an old gobbler without sitting comfortably atop a little foam seat.

Caring For Your Camouflage

You can easily spend several hundred dollars piecing together a "turkey hunter's tuxedo." Here's how to reap the most from your camouflage investment.

Patterns are heat transferred onto modern synthetic garments, which are "the coming thing in camouflage," says Trebark creator Jim Crumley. "Synthetics cost more than cottons, but you can wash them forever and they won't fade or shrink."

Camo patterns are roller-printed onto cotton pants, shirts, and jackets, which are affordable and popular with spring gobbler hunters. To minimize the fading and shrinking of cotton clothes, purchase a large plastic bucket, fill it with water and add a box of baking soda. When your camouflage items become sweaty and soiled, slosh them in the mixture and soak them overnight. The next day, wring out the clothes and hang them outside to drip dry.

The constant pounding of a washing machine causes cotton camouflage to fade. A hot dryer beats the earth-tone colors off garments and causes them to shrink. But if you choose to launder your field uniform in machines, here's how to minimize the damage.

Set your washer to the cold water and gentle cycles. Use only baking soda or one of the UV-free "hunter's detergents" on the market today.

Before washing, turn your camouflage clothes inside out and button up shirts and zip pants. Remove garments quickly from the washer and hang them outside to dry. If you use a dryer, set it on low heat, keep your camo turned inside out and get it out of the machine as quickly as possible.

Today's cotton camo is treated to be extremely colorfast, but fading will occur over time. Slight fading can cast a natural blue on certain camouflages that make them blend even more effectively in certain light conditions. In turn, too much fading can lessen a pattern's detail and make it stand out too much. Contrast of colors is what you desire. When your camouflage fades enough to lose that contrast, it's time to get a new turkey hunting suit.

Boots

Simply tailor your footwear to the terrain you hunt. When chasing Easterns or Merriam's in mountainous regions, stout leather boots are the ticket. I find that modern "bobbed" soles allow you to climb rugged ridges like a billy goat. You also need thick leather boots when hunting Rio Grandes in Texas, where the ground is rough and rocky and many bushes wear thick, sharp thorns.

Check out the Russell Moccasin Company's custom-made turkey hunting boots. You can tuck your pants inside them to ward off ticks and other pests. The Russell's are surprisingly cool, and their 16-inch Cordura uppers provide peace of mind in snake country.

When calling Easterns or Osceolas in swamps and other water-logged areas, I wear knee-high rubber boots. These keep your feet fairly dry (I say fairly, because your feet will sweat when encased in rubber) when crossing creeks and backwaters to get to a gobbling turkey.

Always tuck your camo pants inside of any type of boots. This keeps ticks, chiggers, spiders and other pests from crawling up your legs and finding an unwelcome home. One time in Mississippi, I failed to tuck my pants and paid a heavy price. A hundred seed and deer ticks ate me up, a none too pleasant experience I can assure you. And a potentially dangerous one in this day and age of Lyme disease and other tick-borne illnesses.

A note here: Spray your tucked pants and boots with an insect repellent containing the chemical DEET.

I have worn one set of boots—specially designed Turkey Hunters from the W.C. Russell Moccasin company of Berlin, Wisconsin—on 90 percent of my spring hunts across the country during the past 10 years. My battle-scarred Russells, which feature double-stitched leather bottoms and 16-inch camouflage Cordura uppers, are still going strong. They leak a little, but today's new models have Gore-Tex liners.

I love the custom-made Russells for three reasons. One, it is easy to tuck your pants inside of them to keep ticks and other pests at bay. Two, while Russells are not snake boots per se, they are tall, tough and thick enough to turn fangs, which provides peace of mind when hunting where rattlers and cottonmouths slither (common in many parts of southern turkey range). Finally, Russells make you look like a serious gobbler chaser! A pair of custom-fitted Russells will cost you plenty, but they will last forever. I believe you will love them.

Topos, Aerials & Other Navigational Tools

Topographic maps and aerial photographs are invaluable but often overlooked turkey hunting tools. Topos provide a graphic representation of a quadrangle of the earth's surface. Aerials provide a bird's eye view of a piece of turf.

Topo maps are a valuable investment. Use them to stay found and predict where spring gobblers will roost, travel and strut.

These charts not only allow you to "stay found" and hunt safely, they also provide valuable clues as to where spring gobblers will likely roost, feed, water and strut. Whenever you plan to hunt big, new country, you simply must obtain maps and aerials. But even if you have been hunting a chunk of land for years, I urge you to make the minimal investment in charts.

In the latter case, maps and aerials can reveal what you have been doing wrong all those spring seasons. You can read the charts to see how you made ill-fated approaches to roosted and strutting turkeys. On the bright side, you can use maps and aerials to plot strategic new courses and setups that will dramatically improve your odds of calling in gobblers.

Specific details for scouting and hunting with maps and aerials are found in Chapter 5. Here's a little background on the charts and how to obtain them.

For more than a century, the Interior Department's U.S. Geological Survey (USGS) has planned, created and revised topographic maps of the United States. Today, some 60,000 topos cover every square inch of the nation.

The USGS produces topographic maps in five scales, each with a different-sized quadrangle. The largest-scale topo map—designated as either 1:24,000 or 7.5 minute series—is the most useful for turkey hunters. A 7.5 minute map is highly detailed. One inch represents approximately 2,000 feet, and a quad covers 50 to 70 square miles.

The USGS offers catalogs and indexes of topographic maps for all 50 states. You simply review a state catalog and choose the specific topo(s) you need. Map catalogs and indexes, which are free upon request from the USGS, come with order blanks and price lists (most topos cost under $5). To order state catalogs and specific topo maps, contact: U.S. Geological Survey, ESIC, 507 National Center, Reston, VA 22092 (800) USA-MAPS.

Ordering topographic maps from the USGS can take weeks. Since you'll need a topo in a hurry when hunting new country, check local sources for map availability. Many county and state agencies that deal in land management (soil and water conservation agencies, forestry departments, etc.) sell topographic maps. Local bookstores and gun shops may stock them.

The USGS also sells aerial photographs for most areas of the United States. Photoimages of specific tracts of land are also available from commercial aerial survey firms across the country. Check your phone book under "Photographs—Aerial."

In addition to maps and aerials, you need a compass, especially when trekking in unfamiliar turf. Many turkey hunters carry a compass in vast mountainous regions, but for some strange reason leave it at home when hunting flatlands. This is a big mistake! I've been turned around for hours in Southern hardwood bottoms and swamps, where there are few prominent landmarks and every thing looks the same. You can waste a lot of prime hunting time and maybe even get lost by failing to carry a compass. Keep one in your vest and learn how to use it.

Global Positioning System (GPS) devices are becoming all the rage with outdoor enthusiasts today. These small, battery-powered units accept and decipher navigational data beamed from defense satellites that orbit the earth. Although they are expensive, GPS units intrigue me, and I have tinkered with a few in the spring woods.

The biggest and most obvious advantage of a GPS device is that it will get you from point A to B and back again when walking in miles to turkey hunt at dawn, or when hiking out at twilight after roosting trips. Interestingly, having put a gobbler or two to bed, you can select strategic set-up trees, key them into a GPS device and return within feet of the trees in pitch-black darkness the next morning. This would alleviate the chance of missing your mark and stumbling beneath a roosted tom's tree, something that is not difficult to do. I've spooked my share of gobblers that way, and you probably have too.

I believe GPS units will continue to increase in popularity with hunters. And like computers and other electronics, GPS prices are likely to fall, making them more affordable for the majority of turkey hunters. Check out one of the high-tech toys. I think you might like it.

Binoculars

For some odd reason, many turkey hunters fail to tote a binocular. Granted, spring gobbler hunting is primarily a listening game, but there are countless opportunities to spot turkeys before they see you and spook.

A quality compact, 7X or 8X binocular is necessary when chasing Merriam's and Rio Grandes. It is not uncommon to spot western turkeys traveling, feeding, watering and strutting miles away in open canyons, prairies and meadows. And since the quarry often covers a lot of country each day, glassing the birds and the

A compact, 7X binocular is required gear in western turkey country, and a boon when hunting Easterns and Osceolas around fields, clearcuts, burns, logging roads and other openings. Anytime you can glass a gobbler before setting up, you enjoy a huge tactical advantage.

surrounding countryside to plan strategic approach routes and setups is often the key to success.

But a compact glass also comes in handy when hunting Easterns and Osceolas around fields, clearcuts, burns, logging roads and similar open areas. In Florida one evening, crack Osceola guide Jim Conley and I set out to roost a gobbler for the next dawn's hunt. Walking across a sun-baked pasture toward a cypress swamp, we froze in unison and melted into the sandy earth. I raised my compact binocular to examine five Osceola turkeys busily chasing supper.

Through my 7X Leupold, I watched three hens and a pair of crimson-headed jakes skittering around and nabbing grasshoppers. "Hens and jakes," I whispered to Conley. Then something truly magnificent strode into focus. I gasped, "Wait a minute, big gobbler. Black as tar. Huge white head. Can't see spurs, but his beard is dragging the ground."

"I know where he's gonna roost," Conley smiled. Without taking my binocular off the first Osceola tom I had ever seen, I answered, "Then I know where we'll be hunting tomorrow morning!"

We killed that turkey, but there is a more important moral to the story. In any type of terrain, look for spring turkeys as intensely as you listen for them. When you spot a distant bird, ease your compact binocular from your vest to determine hen, jake or longbeard. If it is the latter, you obviously have a tremendous tactical advantage. Continue to glass the gobbler to predict his travel route, then maneuver into prime calling position.

Decoys

I sometimes carry three decoys in my vest—two hens and a jake—though I have mixed feelings about using them. As discussed later in this book, decoys can be great for bowhunting, as they attract a gobbler's attention while you draw an arrow. Fakes can also be excellent for duping toms in fields and other open spaces.

On the other hand, I have seen times when decoys spooked gobblers, or at least hung them up out of shooting range. It is curious, really, because some toms like the look of decoys (often running in to "breed" a fake hen or spur a foam jake) while other gobblers simply abhor them. Also, I've seen hens turn away from decoys and carry the gobblers strutting behind them off into the sunset. The use of decoys depends on the mood of the individual turkeys.

But if you live and hunt in one of the 40-plus states that permit decoys for spring hunting, it pays to stake them out on occasion. Foam dekes from Feather Flex, Carry Lite and other manufacturers

Modern foam decoys either twirl in the breeze or feature strings that you pull to move them—this adds realism to your calling setup. Decoys are certainly not foolproof, but can lure longbeards on occasion.

are easy to roll up and pack in the rear pouch of a turkey vest. In the field, they sit atop aluminum stakes and twirl around in the slightest breeze, adding motion and realism to your setup.

Last spring I used a Higdon motion turkey decoy for the first time. At first I was skeptical of the Finisher Flirt, which features nylon string running from a plastic crappie reel to the decoy's neck. But then I decided what the heck, I'll try it. I staked the fake hen in a sandy southern road bed and unrolled the string until I reached my calling setup.

As I yelped, I tugged on the string to raise and lower the decoy's head. To my surprise and delight, a pair of hens and three Eastern longbeards pranced within 10 yards of my "feeding" hen. I dropped one of the big gobblers with a charge of Number 4 shot.

I am now a believer in the motion decoy! It is not foolproof, but it will work for you on some spring hunts.

Turkey Wings

The best wing to pack in the rear pouch of your vest comes from a hen turkey shot during an either-sex fall season. A wing is most effective for simulating a cackling hen flying down from the roost. You can also use a wing to create subtle turkey sounds, such as a hen turning and preening on her limb at dawn (more on this in Chapter 12).

Every serious spring hunter should carry and use a wing, for it adds realism to your early-morning calling routines. But heed this safety precaution: Flap and tap a wing sparingly on private ground and never use it on heavily hunted public areas, where some reckless idiot might take the movement of your wing for a gobbler flashing in the foliage.

Carry a turkey wing to simulate the sounds of a hen turning on her limb and flying down at dawn.

Blinds

Brell-Mar Products of Jackson, Mississippi, and several other manufacturers offer camouflage blinds for turkey hunting. Blinds provide the ultimate concealment and are excellent for archers who must raise up, turn and draw arrows as gobblers approach. Commercial hides can also be good for bowhunters or shotgunners who set up and "cold call" for hours in hopes of luring a sporadically gobbling turkey during the midday hours.

I rarely use a blind, preferring a more mobile hunting strategy. But there is no doubt a hide can help you bag a turkey on occasion. Choose a camouflage mesh model that attaches to aluminum poles. Such a blind is lightweight, highly portable and can be assembled in less than a minute. Your blind should be about three feet high with an open top that provides good concealment but maximum visibility.

Pruning Shears

Find a spot in your turkey vest for a pair of hand clippers. At each calling setup, use them to trim away limbs, saplings, vines or brush that might impair your vision or impede the smooth swing of

If you breast out your gobblers, a knife with a sharp, three-inch blade is the only tool you'll need. A little saw blade comes in handy for building a brush blind or trimming saplings from a calling setup.

your bow or shotgun. In early-spring woods with little sprouting foliage, I often use shears to clip several leafy limbs or evergreen boughs, which I then stake four feet in front of my set-up tree for extra concealment. Once a gobbler is in hand, shears make removing wings and legs a breeze.

The Finishing Touches

I carry not one but two Mini-Mag flashlights in my vest. If I lose one or its bulb or batteries die, I can still negotiate the predawn woods. A note here: Point a Mini-Mag's tiny beam straight down to the ground to access the pitch-black woods and minimize the odds of spooking roosted turkeys. Whenever possible, cut your light and go by the creamy glow of the moon.

Pack a quality folding knife, which serves a multitude of purposes afield. If you are like me and breast out 90 percent of the turkeys you harvest (the halves of white meat are sumptuous roasted and mouth-watering when cut into thin strips and grilled or fried), a knife with a finely honed, three-inch blade is the only field-care tool you need.

Carry a small first-aid kit in a vest pocket. Band-Aids and antiseptic come in handy for minor cuts and scratches. Be sure to stuff your kit with Excedrin or Tylenol. Turkey hunters who rise at 4:00 a.m. day after day are prone to develop headaches. And hammering away on a mouth diaphragm at crafty gobblers who give you the slip will only increase the pain!

Since soft showers and booming thunderstorms are common in spring gobbler country, you need to carry rain gear in your truck or vest pouch. An expensive Gore-Tex suit in your favorite camo pattern is best, but a lightweight jacket or poncho is adequate for waiting out the rain.

Carry a plastic water bottle. Water keeps you hydrated in the hot spring woods and refuels your saliva when yelping a lot on a mouth diaphragm.

Finally, pack extra prescription eyeglasses or contact lenses if you need them (something many hunters fail to do). If you break your glasses or if a twig plucks a contact from your eye, quickly switch to your backup and refocus on the gobbler pursuit.

Diverse calling is the key to consistently luring longbeards. If a finicky or call-shy gobbler shuns your high-pitched mouth yelping, switching to a raspy box or slate might bring him running.

Chapter 3

The Caller's Arsenal

Hooooooaaaawww. Gaaaarrrraoobbbble. The sweetest music in all of nature responded to my owl call.

Slipping through the dark creek bottom, I cut loose another mighty hoot. Dead silence, but no problem. I pulled out a crow call—*caw, caw, caw.* The turkey boomed a second gobble from his limb 200 yards away. I flinched and sneaked into calling position. Snuggled against an oak tree, I waited for pink to brush the eastern horizon. I then placed a hickory peg on a slate cup and scratched out *keeowk, keeowk, keeowk. Gaaarrrraoobbbble, gaaaarrrraoobbbble!* When a hot turkey double gobbles at your tree call, it is time to shut up and play the waiting game.

The crown of the crimson-orange sun peeked over the treetops, and I heard the thumping of the tom's great wings as he pitched down. *Keeowk, keeowk, keeowk* pleaded my slate. The gobbler ignored me this time. I figured he was one of those long-spurred, battle-wise warriors.

I pulled out my box—*keeawk, keeawk, kakakakakaaaa, puk, puk, puk, puk.* The turkey rattled the foliage with a thunderous gobble and moved my way.

Rays of sunlight slanted into the mist-shrouded oaks, turning the Alabama woods into my own little piece of heaven. Then the old tom appeared, rising from the earth like a grand apparition. His ivory head glimmered. The new sun danced on his coppery fan and sprinkled his onyx breast with reds, greens and golds. Like every wild turkey that struts into range, this bird was the most magnificent creature I had ever laid eyes on.

With the turkey spinning in all his gaudy splendor 35 yards away, I popped a short burst of air across a mouth diaphragm. The gobbler scissored in his fan and craned his red-blue neck in my direction. With much glee and a tinge of sadness, I pressed the shotgun's trigger.

Single-note flutter on an owl hooter. A trio of caws from a crow call. Tree yelp on a slate. Excited yelp, cackle and fly-down clucks from a box. Soft cluck on a diaphragm to break the monarch's strut. Seven distinctly different calls, all eliciting positive gobbler responses. A thrilling hunt and one of my finest southern longbeards ever in hand.

I am a firm believer that diversity is the key to consistently calling spring gobblers. It plays off the theory that all wild turkeys have distinct little voices. Some hens are high-pitched and whiny, while others sound raspy and squawky. A wide range of hen talk falls in between. Toms often key in to one particular type of hen vocalization that strikes their fancy.

Now this is not to say that a lovesick gobbler will not breed the first hot little hen that gives him the golden opportunity, regardless of how she sounds. He most certainly will! But the fact remains that turkeys often prefer one type of voice over another, just as we humans do.

Mastering a variety of calling devices also gives you a leg up when dueling what is commonly referred to as "call shy" gobblers. Before pecking from their eggshells, wild turkeys learn to recognize the vocalizations of their mothers and siblings. This innate ability to "voice imprint" sticks with the birds throughout their lives. It enables mature toms to recognize various types of hen talk, be it coming from the real thing or a mocking hunter.

Let's say you work a gobbler one morning with a high-pitched diaphragm call. If he makes the major effort to move 100 yards in your direction but fails to see a hen, he will be leery to return the following day to check out those same high-pitched yelps.

A tom cannot reason that the "naked yelping" he heard was you, a hunter poised to steal his beard and spurs—he would neither gobble at your calls nor drift toward them if that were the case. But I do think a turkey can reason, "Been over there and done that, but found no hen." This can cause him to hang up or actually move away from one style of calling day after day.

In this case, all you might need to do is leave that high-pitched diaphragm in your vest, and switch to a raspy slate or box call. Thinking a new, sweet-talking hen has entered his breeding zone, that once finicky gobbler might trip over his beard running into your yelps.

Finally, one brand of calling device, generally a mouth diaphragm manufactured by a call company close to home, is often highly popular in a region, used by 80 percent of the hunters who canvass the spring woods. Gobblers are hammered with nearly identical-sounding raspy or whiny yelping day after day.

Carrying a variety of calling devices with unique tones allows you to mimic multiple hens with distinct little voices.

In desperate need of love and affection, a tom struts in to check out the calling, only to be spooked by a moving hunter. Heaven forbid, he may honor the popular call and then be forced to head-duck a booming charge of Number 4 shot one morning. You can bet that gobbler will reason, "Been over there and done that, and no way I'll ever return!" You will need to switch to a new call with unique tone and rasp to fool such a skittish old devil.

So there are many reasons why you should learn to master a minimum of three locating devices and all six types of turkey calls—diaphragm, box, slate, push-peg, tube and wingbone. Carry this arsenal (it sounds like a lot of stuff, but calls are small and easily organized in your vest) and use each device freely. You'll have the ability to mimic every call in the wild turkey's vocabulary. More importantly, you'll sound like multiple hens with unique voices—often what it takes to bring a finicky or call-shy longbeard running to your calls.

Locator Calls

Owls, crows, coyotes and hawks are mortal enemies of wild turkeys. Then why in the world would a gobbler roar at a predator's call, thus revealing his presence and putting his feathers in peril? To me, it is one of the curious wonders of nature.

Harold Knight's reed-style owl hooter can shock gobbles from roosted turkeys across the country. Owl hooters work best at dawn and dusk, but can pull gobbles from strutting toms in the middle of the day on occasion.

Fact is, a turkey does not want to gobble at a predator's voice, he simply can't help it sometimes. The sharp, attacking calls of his foes simply serve as stimuli that often (not always) make a breeding tom "shock gobble." You play off this by using locator calls to pull gobbles from roosted or strutting toms. Their locations betrayed, you then move in to work the turkeys.

Mimicking the raucous hoots of a barred owl is the most popular way to shock gobbles from turkeys at dawn or dusk. If possible, use your natural voice, grunting air from deep in your chest to simulate the one- to eight-note hoots of an owl. I have hunted with some of the best voice hooters in the country, and they make an amazing number of turkeys gobble.

Many hunters, myself included, are not very good voice owlers. For us, a plastic owl call with a mouthpiece, internal reed and a sounding barrel is the way to go. Reed-style hooters are loud and versatile, allowing you to simulate a wide range of owl talk, from single-note flutters to long, aggressive laughs.

I typically use Knight & Hale's Shock Gobble Owl, though many call companies make excellent models. The key to using any brand

A crow call is my favorite locating device. Primos' rubber-tipped Power Crow is loud and versatile.

of hooter is to force air from deep in your chest up into the reed of the call. To muffle or increase a hooter's volume, vary your hand placement around the call's barrel. Closed fingers muffle your hooting, while a loose hold maximizes volume.

Read the instructions that come with your hooter and practice a lot, for these devices can be moderately difficult to get the hang of. During preseason scouting, hit the woods at dawn and dusk and listen to barred owls hooting away. Whether you plan to voice call or use a reed-style hooter, there's no better way to learn the language than from the masters themselves.

An owl hooter is required gear in Eastern turkey range, but carry one regardless of where you hunt. I've had Rio Grandes and Merriam's hammer hoots in areas where there wasn't a live barred owl for a thousand miles. Remember, it is the shock quality of a locator call, not its actual sound, that causes toms to gobble.

My favorite locating de-vice is a crow call, which can pull gobbles from turkeys anytime of day. A wooden or plastic crow call is easy to use—you simply blow air into its mouthpiece and over its internal reed. The crow's three-caw "come here" call often provides all the shock power you need at dawn. More aggressive rallying or fighting crow calls may be required to force strutting birds to gobble in the middle of the day.

Many companies produce excellent crow calls. One of the best is Primos' Power Crow. The call is loud and attacking. You can bite into the call's unique rubber-tipped mouthpiece to vary the tone and volume of your caws.

Forever searching for the ultimate gobbler locator, my friend Mark Drury of M.A.D. Calls recently introduced an innovative device. Patterned after a silent dog whistle, Drury's Dead Silence has a peak tone of 15,000 hertz (humans hear up to around 8,000 Hz). Drury claims the call's high-frequency notes, all but inaudible to humans, can be heard by roosted gobblers 400 yards away.

"It's hard to fathom the effectiveness of Dead Silence until you experience it, I'll say that," Drury told me. "But we all know that high-frequency sounds like a jet flying over can shock turkeys into gobbling. This just fits in with that."

Hunting a farm in Missouri last spring, Drury and I encountered a turkey gobbling his head off on an adjoining piece of posted property. Since going after the gobbler was not an option, I decided to do a little field-testing.

"Hit him with your whistle," I said to Drury. "I want to see if that thing works."

He pierced the air with a "silent" locator call, and the turkey roared back. Drury whistled six times, eliciting four gobbler responses.

Interestingly, there was a delayed reaction to Dead Silence. We would blow our whistles and the turkey would not hammer right back, as is often the case with an owl or crow call, but wait a second or two before gobbling. "Might have something do with the call's high-frequency sounds," Drury offered.

Mark Drury says gobblers roosted 400 yards away can hear the high-pitched notes of his Dead Silence locator call. I've shocked gobbles from several toms with Drury's whistle, which is neat because it doesn't betray your presence to turkeys or other hunters in an area.

I don't know about that, but I do know from personal experience that Dead Silence works on occasion. It won't make a gobbler roar every time, but then no locator call will. The whistle is just another device you might want to add to your bag of turkey hunting tricks.

Finally, consider packing a coyote howler and a hawk call. Both take up little room in your vest, are easy to blow and can make fired-up toms gobble.

In Chapters 6 and 7, you will find strategies for keying locator calls to dawn and midday turkey hunts. One thing mentioned in the following pages is worth noting again here.

I think far too many hunters overuse locator calls. Rather than blasting away on an owl or crow call first thing in the morning, give toms the opportunity to gobble on their own. This allows you to make a silent, inconspicuous approach toward a bird's roost tree. If no gobblers roar as pink strokes the skyline, probe the woods with moderately aggressive locator calls and go from there.

Turkey Calls

Now let's examine the spring gobbler hunter's most coveted toys. In the following sections, you will find descriptions of the six types of turkey calls, along with pros and cons and helpful tips on using each device.

Mouth Diaphragms

Diaphragms, a.k.a. "mouth yelpers," feature thin latex or prophylactic rubber reeds crimped into aluminum, horseshoe-shape frames. A tape skirt covers the frame and serves as an air seal when you blow a diaphragm.

Mouth yelpers, which date back to the 1860s, are undoubtedly the most popular turkey calls on the market today. Hundreds of models are available. I can personally attest to the quality and effectiveness of Primos, Perfection, M.A.D., Quaker Boy and Knight & Hale diaphragms. Many other call companies make excellent models.

The best mouth yelpers are individually hand stretched to produce consistent tones. Diaphragms typically feature one to four rubber reeds. The fewer the reeds, the higher the pitch and the lower the

Diaphragms feature aluminum frames, rubber reeds and tape skirts that act as air shields when you blow the call. Single- or stack-frame models with one to four reeds are available from many turkey call companies.

volume of the call. For example, a single-reed diaphragm is good for soft, clear-toned clucks and tree yelps, while a four-reed call is designed for loud and raspy yelping and cutting.

Many diaphragms have cut or notched reeds, which add lots of rasp to the calls. Some mouth yelpers have two or even three aluminum frames stacked 1/16 of an inch apart. On these type of calls, the rubber reeds never touch.

I use many varieties of diaphragms, but find myself sticking to a stack-frame when a gobbler battle really heats up. I typically blow Primos' True Double, which is easy to control. The call does not slip around in your mouth, and since the reeds never stick together, you get true notes all the time. A stack-frame call provides lots of rasp, which I find makes many toms gobble like crazy.

Some turkey callers, especially those with small mouth palates, do not like the feel of stack-frame calls. If this is you, choose one of the hundreds of thin, single-frame diaphragms on the market.

Mouth yelpers have many advantages, the most touted of which is hands-free operation. You can run a diaphragm while synchronizing your shotgun with an incoming gobbler.

Pros

The most touted advantage of the mouth yelper is its hands-free operation. You simply sit tight and ease your shotgun barrel or bow into position while clucking and yelping on a diaphragm to an incoming gobbler.

Also, mouth calls are obviously not affected by mist or rain. They are the best choices for hunting on nasty spring mornings.

Since there are literally hundreds of diaphragm models available, each with a unique tone, you can master five or six mouth calls to mimic multiple hens with distinct voices. Remember, we are striving for diverse calling here.

And to that end, diaphragms are the most versatile calls going. You can run the gamut of hen vocalizations on your favorite mouth yelper, uttering soft, melodious purrs and scaling up loud, raspy cutting.

Cons

A few people with "gag reflex" cannot use mouth calls. And while diaphragms can be difficult to master, we are not talking rocket science here. With practice, any turkey hunter with a reasonably musical ear can learn to use mouth yelpers effectively.

Diaphragm Calling Tips

Place a diaphragm into your mouth with the frame's open end pointing outward. If you use a multi-reed call, put the short reed on the bottom. Tongue the call up into your palate and position it halfway between your front teeth and the back of your mouth. You can trim the tape skirt a little with scissors, but be careful—too much cutting can affect your air seal and ruin a call. You can also bend the aluminum frame(s) slightly to ensure a tight palate fit.

The key to using any type of diaphragm is jaw movement. Huff air up from your chest and across the call's reed(s) while raising and lowering your jaw. All people call differently. Some exhibit lots of jaw movement, while others show very little. But you must raise and lower your jaw to some degree to reproduce realistic turkey talk.

To yelp, you must learn to instinctively tighten and loosen the pressure of your tongue to make a diaphragm call "roll over." This produces the two-note *keeowk, keeowk, keeowk*. It is easy to do if you move your jaw!

To cluck, simply say the word "puck," popping a short burst of air over the call's reed(s). To purr, flutter your tongue or lips. Purring is the hardest hen vocalization to perfect on a mouth yelper.

Master yelps and clucks, and you will lure your share of spring toms. But remember, the beauty of the diaphragm call is its versatility. Practice with a mouth yelper until you can vary your tongue pressure and manipulate air to cackle and cutt excitedly. The more hen vocalizations you perfect on a diaphragm, the more gobblers you will ultimately fool.

Final Notes

Before using a single-frame call with two or more reeds, roll it around in your mouth for several seconds to wet it with saliva. This loosens stuck reeds and allows the call to roll over the first time you yelp. Also, after the season, clean your mouth yelpers and store them in the refrigerator. They should last for several years.

Box Calls

Most long, rectangular box calls are crafted of maple, cherry, walnut, poplar, cedar and other woods. A few modern boxes feature graphite and wood construction. All friction boxes have a handle screwed into one end of the call. You chalk the handle and scrape it over the box's "sounding lips" to mimic a turkey.

These big friction calls date back at least 150 years. Today they are moderately popular, though in my opinion far too few hunters carry and use them. I use a Perfection, M.A.D., Quaker Boy or Lynch box extensively in the spring woods.

Pros

Box calls are easy to use, great for clucking and yelping and excellent for cutting aggressively to locate strutting gobblers at mid-day. Some say the true test of a box is its purring sounds. If you can purr on a box, the call is a finely tuned one.

Cons

Boxes are large and bulky to carry, though many turkey vests feature zippered box call pockets to minimize this problem. A box

A box call is great for clucking, yelping and cutting. Some boxes work best with a vertical hold. For true notes, grasp a box lightly in your palm and work the handle gently with your fingers.

has a tendency to cluck and yelp on its own as you walk, but this is easily avoided. Put a piece of cloth or an abrasive pad between a box's handle and sounding lips, then wrap the call tightly with a big rubber band.

And you might try this trick. I quiet my box by placing an extra camo face mask between the call's handle and sounding lips. If I lose my mask or leave it in the truck, I have another one handy.

You must move both hands to call on a box. But if you set up properly, back to a tree with your knees pulled up into your body, you can hide this movement behind your knees or off to either side of your body. Simply lay down the box as a sharp-eyed gobbler closes in.

If a wooden box call gets wet, it is pretty much useless. On rainy days, carry your box in a plastic bag and use it sparingly.

Box Calling Tips

For some odd reason, most hunters use a white- knuckle grip on a box call. This produces squeaky, unnatural notes. Lay a box lightly in the palm of your hand, and keep your fingers off the sides (covering the sides deadens the call's sounds). Hold the handle lightly on your fingertips and scrape it gently back and forth over the call's sounding lips.

Many boxes work best with a vertical hold. Place the call in your palm, turn your hand sideways and work the handle up and down. To yelp, move the handle an inch or less off to one side of the box and pull it gently toward you. To cluck, place the lid on the call's sounding lip and pop it gently upward. To cutt, hold the box vertically and bear down on the handle to make series of short, fast, irregular clucks.

Final Notes

Box calls are hand-tuned by most manufacturers. If you desire higher or lower pitched notes, you can adjust the handle screw slightly with a screwdriver. My advice to you is that if your box sounds good when it comes from the package, don't fool with it! But you may need to adjust the handle screw after several seasons, as moisture and humidity can affect the wood's grain and alter the sounds of your calls.

Use only dry, wax-free chalk on your box. Many turkey call companies sell specially-designed box chalk. Frequently clean a box's sounding lips and inner handle with an abrasive pad (not sandpaper) to remove chalk buildup. Keep your fingers off the inner handle and lips of a box, as this can add oil to the chalk and affect the call's sound. Rechalk both sounding lips and lid before yelping to a gobbler.

Slate Calls

These friction calls feature wooden, plastic or graphite cups with internal "sounding resonators" and slate, synthetic-glass or even aluminum surfaces. You strike the cups with pegs crafted of hickory, maple, ash, carbon, acrylic or other woods and synthetic materials.

Slate calls date back to the 1880s and are enjoying a resurgence in popularity. I am glad to see it! A huge fan of friction calls, I generally carry at least two cups and three pegs on spring gobbler hunts.

There are hundreds of slate and glass calls on the market today, and the quality control on most of these is top-notch. I will stick my neck out and say that you can pick any slate call off the shelf, learn to use it and fool a bunch of turkeys.

Pros

Slates are easy to use and extremely versatile. Using a wooden peg on a slate surface, which promotes low volume and pitch, is the best way I know to cluck and purr to close the sale with a gobbler. You can also use a wooden or acrylic striker on a glass-surface call (lots of volume and high pitch) to cutt like a banshee to locate distant gobblers. And last spring, I used M.A.D.'s new aluminum-faced Super Aluminator call with a hickory peg to shock gobbles from turkeys strutting more than a mile away.

Cons

Like boxes, slates require hand movement, though you can easily conceal this with your knees or body when you set up correctly. Slate-surface calls and wooden pegs are definitely affected by mist and rain. Switch to a glass call and acrylic striker on damp or wet mornings.

Slate Calling Tips

Don't squeeze or palm the cup, but cradle it lightly on your fingertips. Grasp the peg as if writing with a pencil. Move the striker against the cup at a 70- to 80-degree angle to talk turkey.

To yelp, make dime-size circles or little straight lines without lifting the peg from the call's surface. Work near the call's edge for high-pitched yelps, and move toward the center for raspier notes.

To cluck, pull the striker toward you in short jumps, again not lifting it from the call's surface. Same goes for cutting, though you must bear down on the peg and speed up the jumps to run together fast, irregular clucks.

I carry at least one slate and one synthetic-glass call, along with two or three different strikers, on spring hunts. True slates are dynamite for soft clucking, yelping and purring to close the sale with a gobbler. You can really bear down on a glass call to yelp and cutt aggressively.

Final Notes

Frequently sand slate calls with fine sandpaper or an abrasive pad. Use heavier sandpaper on synthetic-glass calls. (All friction calls come from the factory with the proper sandpaper or abrasive pad.) You must also rough the tip of a wooden striker occasionally to make a slate call ring true, something many hunters fail to do.

Push-Peg Calls

This friction call is comprised of a little wooden or plastic box with an internal, spring-loaded push-peg. The wooden or slate-faced peg strikes a sounding plate inside the box to reproduce turkey vocalizations.

Pros

The push-peg is an easy call to use, but it is not strictly for novices. Some of the best turkey hunters I know use push-pegs extensively. The typically high-pitched calls are great for clucking, yelping, purring and close-range cutting. One-hand operation makes them convenient to run.

The push-peg call is easy to use with one hand, but the device is not strictly for beginners. A push-peg's high-pitched yelps, clucks and cutts drive some gobblers crazy.

Cons

Since these calls are not loud, they are best used for close-in work. By design, push-pegs, with thin sides and internal springs, are not very durable, so find a safe place for one in your turkey vest.

Push-Peg Calling Tips

Hold the call lightly in your hand and push the peg with your forefinger. You can also turn the box around and pull the peg toward you with your other hand to produce louder yelps. To cluck or cutt, I hold the call upright in one hand and tap the peg slow or fast with the palm of my other hand. That's all there is to it!

Tube Calls

These hollow plastic tubes are fitted with latex or silicone reeds. Tubes have been around for over 100 years, but enjoy limited use today. Knight & Hale and Primos make the most popular tubes on the market, although other turkey call companies offer quality models.

Pros

You can cutt loudly on a tube to locate gobblers. Tubes also make nice, hollow yelps, which add yet more diversity to your calling arsenal. I use a tube to challenge toms with aggravated purring and gobbling.

Cons

Tubes have a reputation for being difficult to blow, but I believe most hunters fail to give them a chance. With practice, anyone can yelp, cluck, cutt and gobble on a tube. Tubes require hand movement around the face that is not easily concealed, so you must consider this when a keen-eyed gobbler is close.

Tube Calling Tips

The key is to position your bottom lip properly against a tube's reed (all tubes are made a little differently, so mastering this takes some trial and error.) Don't blow too hard, just huff air from your chest. I find that tipping a tube slightly up helps to position my lips properly for clucking and two-note yelping. Pop hard, fast bursts of air against a tube's reed to cutt. To rattle or gobble, run rapid-fire, fluttering air over the reed.

A tube call tosses hollow yelps into the mix. You can also purr aggressively and gobble on a tube to challenge dominant toms.

Wingbone Calls

The wingbone, or suction yelper, is traced back nearly 200 years in the South. The small radius bone from a hen turkey's wing serves as the call's mouthpiece. A larger bone, piece of hollow wood or a cow horn acts as a sounding bell.

Pros

Hollow, high-pitched yelps from a wingbone carry a long way and can make distant gobblers roar. Also, a traditional wingbone adds an element of romance to a spring hunt. A cow horn wingbone was one of the first calls Tom Stafford, a fine man and one of the best old-time turkey hunters in Virginia, showed my dad and me how to use three decades ago. Mr. Tom is gone now, but he is with us in spirit every time a gobbler bellows at our cow horns.

Cons

You are pretty much limited to yelps and clucks with a suction device, though some people can kee-kee on them. Some hunters find

When you kiss into a wingbone call, the clear-toned yelps carry well and can make distant gobblers roar. Using a traditional wingbone adds an element of romance to the spring hunt.

wingbones difficult to master. Actually, most people never get the chance to tinker with a wingbone because few call companies manufacture them today. Perfection's In-ticer, which features a plastic mouthpiece and a wooden barrel, is a modern spinoff of the old wingbone. You might run across a custom craftsman who makes a few wingbones each year. If so, purchase one and give it a try.

Wingbone Calling Tips

Simply kiss or smack your lips gently into the call's mouthpiece. It takes awhile to find the right lip depth and position. I generally sound the best when I place a wingbone near one corner of my mouth.

Gobbler Calls

Mimicking the hard, attacking gobbles of male turkeys can be an excellent locating technique, sometimes setting off a chain reaction of gobbling from roosted birds at dawn. This is especially true when hunting Rio Grande and Merriam's toms, which often pack into western roosts and hammer the first calling stimulus that floats to their ears.

Also, challenging a dominant tom with aggravated purring and gobbling can be effective. It may change an old turkey's thoughts from breeding hens to running over and kicking the tail feathers of a vagabond tom who has invaded an area.

I like to gobble and purr aggressively on a tube call to locate and challenge toms. But if you don't feel comfortable using a tube, check out Quaker Boy's Gobble Shaker, which features hand-tuned latex reeds inside a rubber housing. Simply shake the call like crazy to gobble. Sounds authentic and works great!

Several years ago, Knight & Hale stood the turkey call industry on its ear by introducing the Fighting Purr system. You simply use a pair of push-peg calls to simulate two toms engaged in a fierce, spur-slashing battle. The theory behind the call is simple: Male turkeys, like men in a bar, should race over to watch two fellows slugging it out.

From a business point of view, the Fighting Purr was, and still is, a grand success. Knight & Hale sold more than 80,000 units the second year, and still sells some 30,000 Fighting Purrs annually. Many other companies offer fight-call systems today.

Does recreating a turkey battle really work? I have called in several longbeards with Knight & Hale's Fighting Purr in recent years. I've also had many gobblers fail to respond to the ruckus. Fight call-

I've called in a few longbeards with Knight & Hale's Fighting Purr system in recent years. Challenging dominant gobblers with fight calls is no magic bullet, but it can work sometimes.

ing is not a magic bullet, but it can definitely work on occasion. So adding a pair of push-pegs to your calling arsenal makes sense.

Video & Audio Calling Aids

Many call companies and outdoor production companies market excellent turkey hunting videos today. There are also some trashy turkey tapes floating around out there, so buyer beware!

The quality films feature not only action-packed spring hunts, but also excellent tips on using various types of locator and turkey calls in myriad hunting situations. Whether you are a novice or a seasoned hunter, you will enjoy these videos and pick up little calling pointers that will help you fill your gobbler tags.

I can vouch for the quality and authenticity of turkey hunting videos from Perfection, Primos, Knight & Hale, Realtree and Drury Outdoors. No fake or embellished stuff here—just 100 percent wild turkey hunting and calling action, as it should be.

Many call companies produce quality turkey hunting videos today. The films feature action-packed spring hunts and excellent advice on using the various turkey calling devices in different situations.

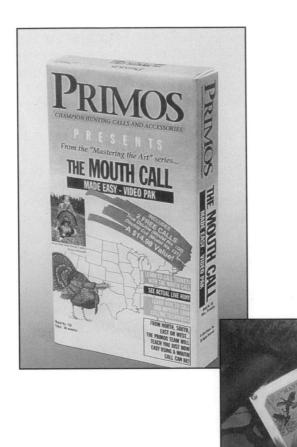

To perfect your calling technique, check out instructional videos and audio cassettes from Primos, Perfection and other companies. Many cassettes feature live hens clucking, yelping and cutting in their natural environment, allowing you to learn the calls from the masters themselves.

From a purely instructional point of view, check out Perfection's "Mastering Slate & Glass Calls" and "Box Calling" videos, along with Primos' "The Mouth Call Made Easy From Start To Finish." These tapes, which come complete with new turkey calling devices, are short on hunting action but long on advanced calling techniques. Expert callers Jim Clay and Will Primos take you step by step through the nuances of using the various types of turkey calls. You cluck, yelp and cutt along as you review the videos to perfect your calling technique.

Primos, Perfection and other call companies also offer audio cassettes of nothing but live wild turkeys clucking, yelping, purring, cackling, cutting and gobbling in their natural environment. You can play these tapes over and over at home and in your truck until the turkey vocalizations become imprinted in your mind. There is no better way than straight from the wild turkey's mouth to learn spirited and diverse calling.

Summary

When you go bass fishing, do you take one crankbait or plastic worm? No, you carry a tackle box full of lures. When the fish aren't hitting one offering, you try another.

Think the same way when you hunt spring gobblers. Carry a complete arsenal of calling devices in your vest. Just as you change bass baits, switch turkey calls. Sooner or later you are bound to get a strike and reel in a big one.

I have turkey hunted across the United States with my battle-worn Remington, which has all the characteristics of the ultimate spring gobbler shotgun.

Chapter 4

Gobbler Guns & Loads

Let's determine the ultimate spring gobbler gun by process of elimination.

First we can dismiss all rimfire and centerfire rifles. Most fish and game departments already have, but a few states still permit rifles for spring turkey hunting. I am no fan of this. A rifleman who stalks along in hopes of getting a long-range shot at a gobbling turkey has no idea if a camouflaged caller is set up in the lush, green foliage nearby. This creates a potentially dangerous scenario.

Besides, spring gobbler hunting is a thrilling chess match of maneuvering and calling, of duping your long-bearded quarry inside of 40 yards and within 35 paces whenever possible. A shotgun (or a compound bow, see Chapter 14) is what you need to get the most pleasure out of the game.

Next we can certainly toss out 28- and 16-gauge shotguns, and the 20 gauge in most instances. These scatterguns, using 2 3/4-inch shells with 2 1/4 to 2 3/4 drams equivalent of powder and 3/4 to 1 1/4 ounces of shot, do not provide sufficient firepower to penetrate a gobbler's head/neck vitals out to 40 yards, especially when angles are tough and there is some ground foliage to shoot through.

This is not to say that a three-inch 20 gauge with the proper loads cannot stop a turkey cold at 30 yards. It can if everything is right. While the 20 gauge is a good choice for young and recoil-delicate shooters, we are striving for the primo gobbler gun here. To that end, the 20 is simply not enough.

To the contrary, the big 10 gauge is certainly more than enough gun for spring toms. Shooting 3 1/2-inch shells with 4 1/2 drams equivalent of powder and 2 1/4 ounces of Number 4 or 6 shot, the 10 gauge can roll turkeys cleanly at 50 yards. But the largest magnum on the market is heavy, bulky, slow-handling, a real shoulder thumper and used by only a thin minority of turkey hunters. All things considered, it cannot qualify as our top choice.

This leaves us with the 12 gauge, and even here we can continue to pare things down. Shotguns with stacked or side-by-side twin barrels, those chambered for 2 3/4-inch shells only, those with tubes over 26 inches long and those with fixed chokes less than full must be tossed aside. You will see why as the discussion progresses.

We end up with a 12-gauge semi-automatic or pump chambered for three-inch (or possibly 3 1/2-inch) magnum shells, wearing a barrel 21 to 26 inches long and choked at least full. Let's examine the specifics of our dream gobbler gun.

I killed this big Rio Grande with the last three-inch shell in my Mossberg 12-gauge autoloader. The third-shot advantage kept me from losing the beautiful turkey.

The Third-Shot Advantage

I like having that third shot, so I use an autoloader, either my battle-worn Remington Model 1100 Special Purpose Magnum or my Mossberg 5500 (since replaced by the company's model 9200). If you are a pump-gun man, more power to you. In skilled hands, a manual shell-shucker fires just as fast as an autoloader and is less prone to jam.

Rarely will you shoot at an incoming gobbler three times. You will either kill him cleanly or miss him cleanly with your first two shots, but sometimes a stunned turkey will surprise you by rolling up and running or flying away. In this case, a third shot can be the difference between a dead gobbler and a lost gobbler.

Several Aprils ago in Texas, I yelped up a big Rio that angled in through a thick patch of mesquite to my left. Having to swing on the turkey, I missed with my first shot but rolled him with the second. As I raced out to claim my prize, the flopping bird regained his composure and with amazing agility catapulted skyward. These gobblers are tough!

As if wingshooting a giant pheasant, I folded the tom with the last charge of Number 5 shot in the Mossberg's chamber. I am not proud of that less than spectacular shooting display, ashamed of it really. But the third shot kept me from committing the ultimate sin of losing a wounded longbeard.

Please, in no way interpret this to mean that since you have a trio of shots, you can sling lead pellets until you finally drop an incoming turkey. Respect our magnificent quarry and strive for quick, clean kills with one well-placed shot to the head/neck vitals. See details on shot placement in Chapter 13.

Besides, each subsequent time that you shoot at a spooked gobbler ducking or flying away, your odds of success diminish rapidly. Each time I sit in the spring woods and count a distant hunter's shots, I read them this way: "One shot, dead turkey. Two shots, maybe. Three shots, messed up big time." This scenario rings true in an uncanny number of situations, though having that third shot can sometimes be a hunt saver.

Barrels & Chokes

Twenty-five years ago, my dad bought me a Remington autoloader with a 30-inch barrel. I killed a lot of gobblers with that gun, but today I cannot imagine waving its long wand around in the spring woods.

The trend toward 21- to 26-inch barrels on turkey magnums has been a grand innovation. Ballistics studies show that shot charges fired from short barrels do not lose significant downrange velocity. But the real beauty of short tubes is that they do not snag limbs and brush as you hike around turkey country. More importantly, compact barrels are easy to maneuver around saplings and through brush as you synchronize with incoming gobblers.

Today's short-barreled turkey magnums offer adequate sighting planes and wield easily around saplings and brush at your calling setups.

*Mossberg and other firearms companies and custom shops offer extra-full tur-
key choke tubes. Test a couple of tightly constricted tubes to see if they improve
your shot patterns.*

After all these years, I am most comfortable with the 26-inch
tube on my Remington 1100. But I also like my Mossberg's even
shorter barrel, which measures 23 1/2 inches from the front of the
receiver to the muzzle. The Mossberg provides an adequate sighting
plane and is a breeze to align on approaching longbeards.

Any choke less than full is taboo in a turkey barrel. As mentioned, gobblers are tough. And many times you must shoot through
some ground foliage out to 40 yards. You need dense patterns.

Most gun companies, including Remington and Mossberg, now
manufacture extra-full turkey chokes that you simply screw into a
shotgun barrel threaded for choke tubes. In addition, custom shops
like Briley and Hastings offer screw-in chokes with even tighter con-
strictions. I think every serious spring gobbler hunter should experiment with several types of extra-tight chokes. When I went to extra-
full tubes in both my turkey magnums, pattern densities improved
dramatically.

Sighting Systems

A single bead on the front of a short shotgun barrel is simply not
enough. You may think the sighting bead is dead-on a turkey's head
and neck when you are actually looking over the top of the barrel.
In the heat of battle, hunters have a tendency to pull triggers and
raise their heads and watch for gobblers to fold. If you fail to cheek
your shotgun when sighting with a single bead, you will shoot over
turkeys.

My gobbler shooting improved tenfold when I added a mid-barrel
bead to my old Remington 1100. By aligning the small mid-barrel

bead with the large white front sight, I know my cheek is down and my shotgun is aimed precisely at a gobbler's flaming red neck and white-crowned head. All modern turkey shotguns feature twin barrel beads, as it should be.

Some turkey hunters swear by adjustable rifle sights on magnum shotguns (the same sights featured on deer-hunting slug guns). Experiment with iron sights, which allow you to align steadily on a gobbler's neck by digging the front bead or blade into the rear "V" sight.

I recently shot a gobbler with a Mossberg magnum fitted with the company's innovative Ghost Ring sight. Here's the deal: You peer through the large "ghosted" aperture of the rear sight and settle the front blade on the head and neck of an incoming turkey. Mossberg claims the Ghost Ring sight is nearly as fast to align as twin barrel beads, only much more accurate.

In my limited experience, I found that to be just the case. I placed the ghost-ringed blade just above the major caruncles of a tom with a 10-inch beard and rolled him cleanly at 38 paces.

In summary, you will probably shoot just fine with twin- barrel beads.

You will probably shoot just fine with twin beads atop your shotgun barrel. But if you're missing turkeys, try a rifle sight or an aperture sight.

But check out rifle or aperture sights if you are missing too many turkeys. If one of these sighting systems enhances your shooting performance, you owe it to yourself and your quarry to go that route.

Scopes For Turkeys

Many serious hunters, especially the old-timers, would rather have a root canal than put a funny-looking optic atop their pet turkey guns.

But just as scopes have come into vogue on deer-hunting slug guns, I think low-power optics might be the wave of the future on turkey autoloaders and pumps.

Scopes offer a couple of major advantages. For starters, unlike twin barrel beads or even rifle sights, there is little margin of error when aligning a scope's crosshair on a gobbler's head and neck. No more failing to cheek your shotgun. No more blotting out a gobbler's neck vitals with a bead or blade at 40 yards, where sight alignment is pretty much a guessing game. Once you sight-in a scoped shotgun, your shot patterns will hit in the same spot every time.

Also, scopes enhance safety. Peering through light-gathering glass at dawn, you can clearly and positively identify your target to be a black-breasted gobbler with a shimmering white head and dangling beard. Any device that makes our sport safer can only be viewed as a positive.

A turkey scope should have low magnification (a variable in the 1.5X-4X range is about right), a minimum of four inches of eye relief (to keep the optic from recoiling back into your face) and a wide field of view (allows you to easily scan wide strips of foliage for incoming gobblers). The most effective sighting system is a crosshair with a small circle, which you place on a gobbler's neck. Bushnell, Pentax, Leupold, Simmons and Tasco offer such scopes for shotguns. All optics manufacturers will probably offer them in the near future.

Known for their rigid support, cantilever and saddle-style mounts are popular for fastening scopes atop hard-recoiling magnum shotguns. But there is a big advantage in using highly positioned "see-though" scope mounts on a gobbler gun.

My friend Jim Clay of Perfection Turkey Calls worked closely with Bushnell in the development of the company's 1.75X-4X Trophy Turkey scope. Here's a guy who has killed a bunch of spring gobblers with twin beads atop his shotgun barrel, but who now uses a scope extensively.

"To me the biggest advantage of a scope comes at 40 yards," Clay says. "You don't have to worry about blotting out a turkey's head and neck with the barrel beads. Just put the crosshair and circle on the turkey's neck, and you know your shot pattern will strike exactly where you're aiming."

I asked Clay about my biggest concern—that a scope's magnification might somehow screw up a hunter's sight picture, making a gobbler look closer than he really is. This could lead to shooting at turkeys out of range.

"That's why I set my scope on its lowest magnification, and always use see-though mounts," the Virginia turkey call maker responded.

I have shot a couple of gobblers with a scope-sighted Mossberg 835 pump. Low-magnification scopes not only enhance sight alignment on a gobbler's head and neck, they also allow you to safely focus on your target. I think you will see a lot more scopes atop turkey magnums in the future.

"This way, you look under the scope and keep your bead on the turkey until he comes into shooting range. Then just move your head slightly up into the scope and take him."

Interestingly, Clay uses his scope and twin barrel beads interchangeably in the spring woods. "I always use the scope when shooting at turkeys 35 to 40 yards away," he says. "For gobblers inside 30 yards, I normally move my eye down to the see-through mounts and use the beads."

I have killed a couple of turkeys with a scope-sighted Mossberg Ulti-Mag 835 pump chambered for 3 1/2-inch shells, one of the hardest-hitting turkey guns on the market. The 12-gauge magnum I used did not feature see-through scope mounts, so here's how I got around my concern of firing at slightly magnified gobblers too far away.

Sitting against trees with the Mossberg leveled across my knees, I watched over the top of the Pentax scope until those gobblers strutted within 35 yards. I then dipped my eye to the scope, aligned the crosshair and pressed the trigger. Both birds went down cleanly.

In summary, I think you will see a lot more scopes on turkey shotguns in the near future. They provide sight-alignment and safety advantages for all hunters, and especially for those with less-than-perfect vision. You might want to try a scope now to get in on the ground floor of the trend.

Shotgun Camo & Accessories

You can purchase a new 12-gauge pump or autoloader that comes straight from the factory with a striking Mossy Oak, Trebark or Realtree finish. Carrying a "concealed weapon" makes you look like a serious turkey hunter! More importantly, you'll spook fewer gobblers.

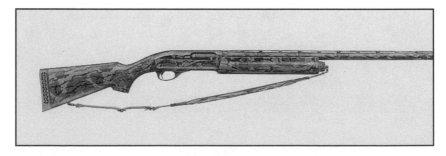

A 12-gauge turkey magnum should wear a no-glare camouflage finish and a carry sling.

Why go to all the trouble of camouflaging your body from head to toe, but then let a little detail, like sunlight flashing on a blued barrel or receiver, reveal your location to a sharp-eyed gobbler? Remember, your shotgun moves more than anything else, and at the most critical time of a turkey hunt. Camouflage your firearm.

While my Mossberg features a Mossy Oak factory finish, my old Remington is covered with either Mossy Oak, Realtree or Trebark tape (since I hunt a lot with all the major camouflage guys, I have to shift back and forth to properly conceal my shotgun). If you have an older-model turkey gun that shoots the lights out, by all means do not trade it in for a new fancy-camoed shotgun. Simply tape your pet magnum to keep from spooking gobblers.

Finally, your turkey gun must wear a carry sling. A 12-gauge magnum weighs a tad over seven pounds. If you hunt seriously, you will cover a lot of ground each spring morning. A sling allows you to tote your shotgun easily and safely.

But don't let a sling cost you a gobbler! Each time you set up to call, clip away any saplings or brush that might snag the sling as you ease your shotgun into final shooting position. And be sure the sling cannot catch your knee when you twist around to align your gun barrel on a turkey's head and neck. Finally, don't allow a sling to dangle around when you shift your shotgun. The little movement might spook an incoming tom.

Turkey Loads

For the spring game, choose only high-grade, three-inch shotshells like those listed in the chart on the following page. Magnum turkey loads from Winchester, Federal, Remington and Activ feature maximum powder charges and two or 2 1/4 ounces of copper- or nickel- plated lead shot with granulated buffering. The loads deliver optimum velocities and consistently dense patterns out to 40 yards, the maximum range at which you should draw down on a gobbler.

Most major ammunition companies offer 3 1/2-inch shotshells for use in Mossberg's popular Ulti-Mag 835 pump. The long loads hold 23 percent more pellets than three-inch shells. Some of the top turkey hunters in the country shoot 3 1/2-inch loads in the Mossberg 835, and, as mentioned, I've killed a couple of gobblers with the combo myself. It thumps your shoulder and cheek at the range, but you'll never feel the recoil when shooting at a gobbler. The Mossberg 835 with 3 1/2-inch loads delivers a lethal dose of turkey medicine when your sighting alignment is true.

Number 4, 5 or 6 shot? The debate rages among serious turkey hunters. Personally, I am a No. 4 or 5 shot man.

I have shot 90 percent of my spring gobblers over the years with Federal's three-inch Premium Magnum Turkey loads with two ounces of copper-plated No.4s. The load patterns densely and consistently in both my Remington and Mossberg autoloaders. I have also tested Federal 4s with grand success in many other models of turkey magnums. I urge you to pattern Federal 4s in your shotgun and use them if they deliver consistently dense patterns.

The remaining 10 percent of my turkeys in recent springs were taken with Winchester's three-inch Double X Magnum Turkey loads with two ounces of No. 5 shot. These loads pattern nicely in my Mossberg semi-automatic. And I like Number 5s because they zing more pellets out there to catch a gobbler's head/neck vitals. To me, No. 5 shot is the perfect compromise for hunters who like the penetration of large 4s, but are intrigued by the benefits of more pellet coverage as delivered by the smaller 6s. I guess that's why the loads are called Number 5 shot!

Ballistics Of Popular Wild Turkey Loads*

Load	Gauge, Shell Length	Powder, Dram Eq.	Muzzle Vel.	Ounces Shot	Shot Sizes
Remington	12, 3 1/2"	Max.	1150	2 1/4	4,6
Premier	12, 3"	Max.	1175	2	4,5,6
Turkey					
Federal	12, 3 1/2"	Max.	1150	2 1/4	4,6
Premium	12, 3"	4	1175	2	4,5,6
Magnum Turkey					
Winchester	12, 3 1/2"	Max.	1150	2 1/4	4,6
Double X	12, 3"	Max.	1175	2	4,5,6
Magnum Turkey					
Activ	12, 3"	Max.	Max.	2 1/4	4,5,6
Penetrator	12, 3"	Max.	Max.	2	4,5,6

*Remington, Federal and Winchester loads are buffered with copper-plated shot. Activ shotshells are buffered with nickel-plated shot.

Patterning Turkey Guns & Loads

Many ammunition and game call manufacturers market life-size targets of a gobbler's head and neck, complete with brain and neck vital areas. These realistic paper targets are excellent for pattering your shotgun with various chokes and loads.

Go to a shooting range, set turkey targets a couple of feet off the ground, back off 20 yards, set up against a tree and level your shotgun across your knees. From this simulated spring turkey hunting position, fire various brands of No. 4, 5, and 6 copper- and nickel-plated shot through full, extra-full and perhaps several more tightly constricted custom choke tubes.

Fired from my Mossberg, Winchester's copper-plated Number 5s produce dense, uniform patterns.

Pattern a variety of three- or 3 1 / 2-inch, 12-gauge loads through full and extra-full choke tubes. When settling on your best load, remember that at least three pellets must penetrate a gobbler's head and neck vitals to stop him cold.

Will Primos

David Hale

Mark Drury

Ronnie Strickland

Toxey Haas

The cross section of the turkey hunting pros I interviewed (shown on this page and opposite) use either Remington or Mossberg 12 gauges and three- or 3 1/2-inch loads of Number 4 or 6 shot. These experts advise you to pattern your shotgun extensively and limit your shots at gobblers to 40 yards.

Repeat the scenario from 25, 30, 35 and 40 yards. Mark distance, load and choke on each target, and then carefully examine the various patterns.

A recent ballistics study commissioned by the Winchester-Olin ammunition company found that to kill a gobbler cleanly, a minimum of three pellets must strike and fully penetrate his brain and/or neck vertebrae. In addition, the study showed that an average of 13 pellets must penetrate a turkey's head and neck to achieve three pellets in the vital zone.

When evaluating loads, use these statistics as a minimum, but strive for more efficient patterns. Modern 12-gauge magnums, custom chokes and improved loads have the potential of throwing denser patterns into a gobbler's head/neck vitals between 20 and 40 yards.

Ron Jolly

Firepower of the Pros

I thought it would be interesting and informative to survey 100 of the best spring turkey hunters I know for their thoughts on shotguns, chokes and loads. Combined, these guys have shot thousands of gobblers—and missed their share—en route to developing what they consider to be the ultimate turkey gun and load.

My poll revealed pretty much what I expected. Sixty percent were pump-gun aficionados: "It's just what I grew up shooting," and "A pump is less likely to jam on a turkey," were common comments. Of the 40 percent who shoot autoloaders, most all use a Remington for its smooth and reliable action.

Ninety of 100 pros shoot shotguns chambered for three-inch shotshells. The remaining 10 percent use Mossberg's Ulti-Mag 835 and 3 1/2-inch loads. "The 835 is deadly on gobblers!" was a common statement.

One thing sort of surprised me: Not as many of the pros have jumped on the extra-full choke bandwagon as I expected. While 60 percent of the hunters have gone to factory or custom chokes with extra-full or even tighter constriction, 40 percent stick with full choke. "Modern turkey loads pattern so tightly, full choke is all you need out to 40 yards," many of the pros told me. "It's easy to miss a gobbler at 20 yards with an extra-full choke and an ultra-tight load."

As expected, I found nearly a 50-50 split on the use of No. 4 and No. 6 shot (a handful of the pros use No. 5s). Most popular comments: "Fours provide the penetration you need to break a gobbler's neck at 40 yards." And "I like the extra pellets of Number 6s." Every pro was quick to say that he chose a load of No. 4 or No. 6 shot based on pattern uniformity and consistency in his chosen shotgun/choke combo.

Every hunter's gun was camouflaged. Most shoot new Remingtons or Mossbergs with factory-camo finishes. But a few are loyal to their old, battle-scarred magnums, which are covered with Mossy Oak, Realtree or Trebark camouflage tape.

Ninety-five percent of the pros use twin-barrel beads to align on a gobbler's head and neck. Five percent use scopes exclusively or sometimes and really like them. "I plan to try a scope soon," was a frequent comment from the bead men, supporting my theory that turkey scopes will come into vogue.

To round out this chapter, here's a sampling of the firepower of the pros, along with sage comments to keep in mind when choosing your ultimate gobbler gun and loads.

Pro Guns & Loads

Hunter	Shotgun	Choke	Load	Comment
Jim Clay, Perfection Calls	Remington 11-87	Briley X-Full	Activ 3" No. 6	"I like an autoloader for a quick second shot if needed. Activ 6s and Briley choke pattern great for me."
David Hale, Knight & Hale Calls	Mossberg Ulti-Mag 835	X-Full	Win. 3 1/2" No. 4	"Go loaded for bear. The 3 1/2-inch shell has more shot for killing turkeys quickly and cleanly."
Ron Jolly, Primos Calls	Remington 870	Full	Rem. 3" No. 4	"No. 4s pattern best in my 870, and I like their penetration."
Mark Drury, M.A.D. Calls	Mossberg Ulti-Mag 835	X-Full	Win. 3" No. 6	"I don't like the recoil of 3 1/2-shells. Three-inch 6s provide great pattern density in my 835."
Ronnie "Cuz" Strickland, Mossy Oak	Remington 870 or Mossberg pump	X-Full	Rem. 3" No. 6	"Both guns are custom-choked for 6s. Barrels have been cut down to 22 inches—very easy to handle in tight spots."
Will Primos, Primos Calls	Remington 870	Full	Rem. 3" No. 4	"No. 4s pattern best for me and have the energy to break a turkey's neck at 40 yards."
Ray Eye, Eye Calls & Videos	Remington 11-87	Full	Win. 3" No. 6	"I don't like too tight of a choke. My setup patterns well and is tight enough at 40 yards, but not too tight at 20 yards."
Toxey Haas, Mossy Oak	Remington 11-87	X-Full	Rem. 3" No. 4	"Loads must be very tight and evenly distributed. No. 4s have lots of energy and penetration at 35 to 40 yards. Because of the small pattern, hold low on a turkey's neck on close-range shots.

Smart scouting involves seeking out as many sources of turkey data as possible. A gray-haired mail lady put me on this big Mississippi gobbler.

Chapter 5

Smart Scouting

The first scenario goes something like this.

You attend your daughter's school play and socialize with the other parents between acts. "Do any turkey hunting," you naturally ask one fellow.

"No, but we sure have lots of birds on our farm," your new best friend replies. "We see and hear turkeys gobbling all the time. Got 1,500 acres. Come on out and hunt this spring."

A second possibility: Flipping through your state-published wildlife magazine, you note a feature article on public hunting areas across the region. Federally managed national forests, state wildlife management areas and accessible timber-company lands are outlined in detail. You decide to check out a couple of the public tracts this spring.

A third potentially expensive but productive situation: Like a growing number of sportsmen in the East, South and Midwest, you decide to bite the bullet and join a hunt club. You shell out hundreds or thousands of hard-earned dollars to hunt Eastern gobblers on several private leases across the county.

These are but three of countless ways to access wild turkey country. I urge you to be creative and investigate as many private and public lands as possible. Having located several places to hunt, here's how to hit the ground running, eliminating unproductive areas and zeroing in on spring gobbler hot spots.

Gathering MRI

First, obtain all available MRI—most recent information—regarding your new turf. Talk with landowners, farm managers and hands, neighbors and other hunters. (The latter are likely to be as tight-lipped as an old gobbler with hens!) Be friendly and casually ask if anyone has heard or seen turkeys in the vicinity.

Ask landowners not only for written permission to hunt, but also for most recent information on turkey densities and patterns in the area.

Other excellent sources of MRI include mail carriers, school bus drivers, game wardens and other folks who travel rural routes daily. These people commonly spot turkeys crossing roads and feeding and strutting in fields. They can put you on gobblers.

One morning in Mississippi, I hunted across 2,000 acres of prime private land without hearing a turkey gobble. Tired and discouraged, I fell out onto a gravel road and trudged back toward camp. A mail lady stopped and offered me a ride. I gladly accepted and climbed into her pickup truck.

As we stopped to drop a stack of bills into some unfortunate soul's mail box, the silver-haired lady pointed out the window and drawled nonchalantly, "I see big old gobblers in that field most every day. That's where you need to hunt."

My eyes brightened and the wheels turned in my mind. Seems the turkeys were using the western fringe of my hunting area, while I was prospecting the east side. Thanks to the mail lady, whom I love dearly to this day, I headed west that afternoon and promptly roosted three longbeards, one of which I killed the next morning.

When gathering MRI, contact a wild turkey biologist in your hunt region. Phone a regional office or the main headquarters of your state's fish and game department. Someone there can put you through to a specialist who can provide turkey density estimates, harvest data and recent brood-production information for specific counties.

This is invaluable stuff, particularly if you plan to hunt big public land, say a 50,000-acre tract managed by the U.S. Forest Service or the Bureau of Land Management. You can heed a biologist's advice to eliminate areas with sparse concentrations of turkeys and zero in on potential gobbler havens.

Mapping Gobblers

Before ever placing a boot in new turkey country, you can get a good feel for the lay of the land by scanning topo maps. Use topos not only to familiarize yourself with an area, but also to predict where turkeys might roost, feed, strut and travel.

Large-scale topos cover specific quadrangles, four-sided areas rimmed by parallels of latitude and meridians of longitude. On these highly specific maps, two inches represents roughly one mile. If your new turf is immense, which it may well be in Eastern, Rio Grande or Merriam's range, you will have to fit together several maps to get a full view of the country.

Topo maps use colors, numbers and contour lines to detail the shape, elevation and terrain features of a tract of land. Here are some map features of particular interest to spring turkey hunters:

*Green designates wooded terrains. White indicates fields, clearcuts, prairies, grasslands and similar open areas.

*Creeks, rivers, ponds, swamps and other bodies of water are shown in blue.

*Red represents primary roads, fence lines and prominent boundaries.

*Contiguous black lines reveal secondary roads (rural route numbers are circled in red). Broken black lines designate logging, ranch and other unimproved roads, as well as trails, gas and power lines and old railroad beds.

*Brown contour lines show the elevation of the country. The closer together the contour lines, the steeper the terrain. Land elevations are indicated with brown numerals.

For starters, read a topo map to zero in on unimproved roads and trails. Locate long series of tight contour lines that indicate prominent ridge lines. Find field edges and creek and river bottoms. Mapping these landmarks is important, for they are your primary travel lanes through turkey country. Walking roads, trails, ridges, edges and waterways, you can scout for fresh sign and listen for gobbling turkeys.

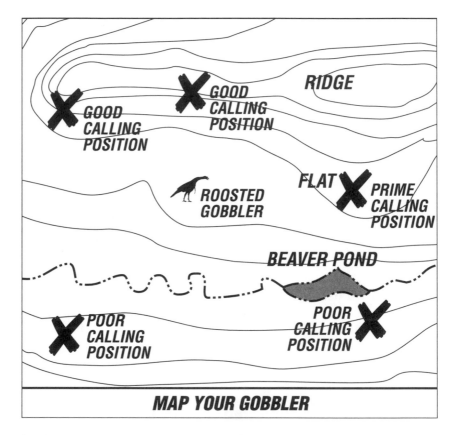

MAP YOUR GOBBLER

Combining map reading with a working knowledge of spring gobbler behavior will enhance your success, as illustrated by this sketch. After roosting this tom one evening, pinpoint his location on a topo map and study the surrounding terrain. Since the bird is roosted north of a creek, you can rule out southern setups — the gobbler will be reluctant to cross the water to come to your calling the next morning. By slipping in from the north, you take the creek out of play and position above the turkey. Any of the three ridge setups could be productive since the gobbler will feel at ease traveling uphill to your yelping. I would probably opt for the flat setup because there's a good chance the gobbler will move up there to strut for hens. On the off chance the tom flies out across the creek, you know from reading your topo map to maneuver south and cross the water before re-positioning to call.

Mapping hunt zones in the Southeast, I often beeline for low-lying areas defined by loose contour lines. You may find Eastern gobblers roosting in creek bottoms, draws or swamps.

In hilly or mountainous terrains, I read topos to target ridges, knolls and bluffs. Hiking to high points of ground not only allows you to listen a long way for gobbler music, but also puts you strategically above birds that tend to roost a third to halfway down hillsides.

Topographic maps are great for locating spring roosts that may be few and far between in Western regions. Amid an expansive sea of prairie or grassland (white on a topo), a small, light-green spot may indicate a pocket of tall ponderosa pines, cottonwoods or live oaks. You will likely find Merriam's or Rio Grande birds roosting in there.

Whenever hunting out West, target blue on your maps. In arid country, creeks, rivers and ponds draw Merriam's and Rios like nails to magnets.

Use a topo map to plot turkey feeding and strutting areas. White-shaded agricultural fields, pastures, clearcuts, power lines and the like provide grains, grasses and insects for hens. These clearings, particularly if secluded and surrounded by green-colored timber, are natural strutting zones for gobblers.

While topo maps are gems for scouting, they are also powerful hunting tools. For example, one morning in the coal country of southern Virginia, I heard a gobbler roar a mile away. I pulled out my map and estimated the location of the old mountain monarch.

I found a jeep trail on my chart and hustled up it to within 400 yards of the turkey. I crow called. The gobbler responded, and again I checked my map. The bird was set up in an oak flat, strutting his tail feathers off I guessed, across a narrow creek.

I hopped the run, which in all likelihood would have hung up the gobbler like a brick wall, and set up within 125 yards of the old boy. I yelped and purred him in 15 minutes later. The "Topo Map Tom" sported an 11-inch beard and 1 1/4-inch spurs.

In addition to topos, aerial photographs are necessary for prospecting turkey country. Visit any serious turkey hunting lodge across the country, and you will find enormous black-and- white aerials adorning the walls. These charts signify the "war rooms" where experienced guides and anxious hunters mingle to lay out battle plans for outmaneuvering crafty gobblers.

The biggest advantage of aerial photos is that they give you a bird's eye perspective of the timber, fields, creeks, draws, logging roads and other terrain features of a tract of ground. Upon roosting a gobbler one evening, you can study an aerial and say, "He is sleeping right there in that patch of timber!" You then scour the photo for an

A muddy or sandy road bed is a good place to scout for droppings, tracks, dust bowls and gobbler strut marks.

old road or trail that permits easy and quiet access to the turkey. You determine how much cover surrounds the bird, and if a creek (potential turkey-hanging hazard) or open field (potential strut zone) looms nearby. Reviewing an aerial, you can evaluate all sorts of things when planning your approach and setup, which obviously gives you a leg up for the next morning's hunt.

Aerial photographs also permit you to distinguish various types of vegetation and trees. This is solid information. For example, you might spy a 10-acre patch of hardwoods nestled amid a sea of thick pines. In the spring, this could be a dynamite place to find feeding hens and strutting toms.

Prospecting Turkey Turf

A biologist might tell you there are tons of turkeys in an area, and your charts might reveal prime habitat for the quarry. But the only true way to determine how many birds are in your hunting area—and precisely where they are living—is to get out there and do some down and dirty scouting.

Wild turkeys preen a lot and discard all sorts of feathers. A fresh, black-tipped breast feather tells you at least one gobbler is in the area.

If the middle toe of a turkey track is more than 2 1/2 inches long, you're hot on the trail of a gobbler.

Your detective work should begin at least a couple of weeks before a spring season commences. It should also continue as you hunt throughout April and May. Such factors as hens going to nest, heavy hunting pressure and new gobblers moving in to take over prime breeding zones where old toms were harvested earlier in the season cause turkey patterns to change. So scout as you hunt to keep close tabs on the gobblers in an area.

During your scouting forays, work a piece of country in some sort of a pattern, perhaps zig-zagging through the woods or walking in ever-widening circles. As you go, here is the specific turkey sign to look for:

Tracks: Both mature gobblers and jakes leave large, three-toed prints. Hen tracks are noticeably smaller. If the middle toe of a track measures 2 1/2 to 3 1/2 inches long, you've found gobbler sign. The middle toe of a hen's track is less than 2 1/2 inches.

Scout for fresh turkey tracks where they are most easily visible—in and around fields, road beds, creeks, ponds and water holes, anywhere the ground is bare and soft or sandy.

Droppings: Gobbler scat is shaped like a fishhook, straight and hooked on one end. Hen droppings are round and spiraled. Fresh droppings are moist and green with a splash of white. Old scat is dry and brown. A field, food plot or old road bed is a good place to check for concentrations of fresh droppings, sign that turkeys are feeding and strutting there.

Dust Bowls: Look for these shallow, oval-shaped depressions in old roads and along the edges of fields and streams. Biologists speculate that turkeys, especially hens, take dust baths not only to repel mites and other parasites, but also to align their feathers. A number of dust bowls in an area may indicate that hens are nesting nearby. Lovesick gobblers are sure to be in the vicinity, especially late in the season.

Strut Marks: Scout for narrow, shallow grooves to either side of a set of large turkey tracks, sign that a gobbler scraped his primary wing feathers along the ground as he strutted. Lots of strutting sign, most easily spotted in an old road bed or along a sandy stream bottom, may indicate a hen-gathering zone that a tom uses each day.

Feathers: Wild turkeys preen a lot and discard all sorts of feathers across their range. Long, white-barred primary wing feathers tell you turkeys are in the vicinity. A wing feather with a rubbed tip indicates the presence of at least one strutting gobbler. Scout for the short, black-tipped breast feathers of toms.

Scratchings: Look for round, jagged scratchings where turkeys raked for old mast, green shoots and insects. Large concentrations of scratchings, such as a rolled up hillside, tell you turkeys are traveling in fairly large flocks, a common occurrence when cold weather dictates a late spring. Small patches of the sign indicate the birds are in small breeding groups or alone. You'll find the most scratchings in early spring. Later, with green vegetation popping up everywhere and insects more active, turkeys scratch less often.

Walk logging roads and field edges and pause on high points of ground to listen for turkeys to gobble. Rather than immediately blasting away on a locator call, keep quiet and give a tom the chance to gobble on his own. This way, he reveals his presence to you without you possibly revealing your presence to him.

Listening For Gobblers

Finding fresh turkey sign is heartening and a prerequisite to success. But the most thrilling way to determine how many gobblers inhabit a piece of hunting turf is to get out there and listen for the birds to bellow from their limbs at dawn and dusk.

Most hunters begin listening a week or so before the spring season opens, and generally this is adequate strategy. But did you realize that you are apt to hear a turkey ringing the woods with his mating call as early as January or February? Anticipating the breeding fun that is just around the corner, some cocky toms get the urge to gobble on warm, sunlit winter afternoons.

It can pay to scout early, particularly when trying to pinpoint turkeys on a big chunk of new ground. If you hear a tom gobble in late winter, you can pretty much bet that you have located a flock of bachelor longbeards. Some of the birds will be treading hens miles away come March, April or May, but more than a few should disperse nearby into your hunt zone.

The most convenient way to listen for turkeys is to drive rural roads that rim the perimeters of a hunting ground. Pull off frequently, cut the engine, step well away from your vehicle (the hissing and twanging of a cooling motor limits your hearing) and listen for your quarry to roar at dawn and dusk.

I have listened with some of the top turkey hunters in the country, a few of which step away from the truck and cup their hands behind their ears, as if this will funnel the sweet gobbling of a distant turkey deep into their ear canals. Following their lead, I have tried cupping, though I'm not sure it really helps. But then, I have the luxury of being able to hear a turkey gobble as far away as any man can. If you have trouble tuning in to long-range gobbles, try cupping your hands and pulling your ears slightly forward. It might give you an auditory edge.

Sometimes the lazy man's way of driving and listening is not an option, such as when scouting big tracts of land with few access roads. In this case, hike down trails, logging roads, field edges and the like at dawn or twilight and pause on high points of ground to listen for gobbles.

Rather than immediately blasting away on an owl hooter or crow call, I like to give turkeys a chance to gobble on their own. This way, they reveal their presence to you, without you revealing your presence to them or other hunters. More on this theory in the following chapter.

But often while scouting, you must locator call to pull gobbles from tight-lipped birds. Start out with a short burst of owl hooting or crow calling. Sometimes a hunter gets so wrapped up in locator calling for 10 seconds or longer that he fails to hear a distant turkey respond. The turkey shoots back a shock gobble, but is drowned out

While either scouting or hunting, my favorite locating technique is to cutt on a friction call. The fast, irregular clucks are loud and aggressive enough to shock gobbles from long-range toms.

by the hunter's dynamic but self-defeating hooting or cawing! Keep your locator notes sharp and short, then perk your ears and listen hard for gobbler music.

I believe the hawk call is an effective but overlooked locating device. Same goes for M.A.D.'s Dead Silence. These calls are shrill enough to shock responses from some turkeys, yet won't cover up a faint gobble.

While either scouting or hunting, the most effective locator call of all, one that you will read about frequently in this book, is hen cutting. For starters, any type of hen talk is the ultimate gobbler stimulus. Cutting just carries things to the next level. The fast, excited clucks are loud and aggressive enough to pull gobbles from the most aloof toms.

Again, keep it sharp but short. A hunter running through a loud, wonderfully realistic, 10-second series of cutts sounds pretty and might score well at a turkey calling contest, but chances are he is flooding out any gobbler that responds.

Once the spring hunting season commences, listening pretty much transforms to evening roosting as hunters try to put to bed gobblers for the next morning's hunt. Gain high vantages at dusk and listen for a gobbler to roar on his own, or try to elicit a response with short bursts of owl hooting, crow calling, hawk whistling or hen cutting. If no gobbler plays the game, that is okay. Sit quietly in the woods and listen for more subtle turkey sounds.

A spring flock, say a dominant gobbler with four hens and a couple of subordinate toms in tow, is noisy. The birds' big feet shuffle leaves as the flock moves into a roosting area. Hens often cluck and yelp spiritedly just before cackling and flying up to their limbs. An old gobbler may or may not gobble at fly-up time, but he may cluck coarsely a time or two.

So listen for the walk and talk of wild turkeys at dusk, and strain to hear the flapping of heavy wings as the birds pitch up to their roosts. This is less exhilarating but actually more revealing that hearing a distant turkey boom a gobble at twilight.

If you hear one set of wings thump up, there's a good chance you have located a solo gobbler. If you hear several sets of wings hammer up into the treetops, you can bet a tom is surrounded by hens. In either case, you can tailor your calling strategies to the task at hand the next morning.

There is an old saying in the South, "A roosted turkey sure ain't a roasted turkey." Boy, is that right on the money. Hearing a tom fly up and possibly even gobble on his limb at dusk seems to be the dream scenario. But calling in and killing the old devil at dawn is something else indeed.

You may return and the turkey might not gobble. Something may have spooked him from his roost during the night. Or he may simply fly down silently, especially if he has hens. And remember, a wild turkey is one of the most unpredictable creatures on earth. A gobbler might roar at all your calls the next morning, then strut defiantly away in the opposite direction.

Roosted sure ain't roasted. Then again, is there a better way to begin a morning hunt than by setting up to call beneath a gobbler you scouted and put to bed the evening before?

For me, toting a big gobbler from the misty morning woods is the essence of spring turkey hunting.

Chapter 6

Gobblers At Dawn

You step out of your truck, click the door shut ever so lightly, load your shotgun and hustle off into the gloom. The last wisps of night air are both humid and chilling. You pause shivering in your sweat to listen from a knoll cloaked in swirling mist and eerie shadows. The predawn woods look and feel like a graveyard.

But then pink glimmers on the eastern skyline. A whippoorwill sings his beautiful melody. Songbirds flitter about, whistling gaily. A half-mile down a ridge a barred owl greets the new day with his odd but enticing, "who cooks for you, who cooks for you all" call. And then there it is, *gaaaarrrroobbbble*, the wonderful rattle of an old turkey's gobble.

Heart pounding like a tiny drum, you sneak quickly toward the gobbler's tree in the gray light. Snuggling into your setup, the monarch roars in your face, his booming gobble cutting to your soul. You flinch, level your shotgun across your knee and pull out your turkey calls. . . .

Gobblers at dawn, the essence of spring turkey hunting. Let the grand game begin!

Where Toms Roost

Knowledge of where turkeys prefer to roost will put you in good maneuvering and calling position first thing each morning. Wherever you hunt, bear in mind that gobblers generally like to sleep in trees located on high points of ground.

Seventy percent of a turkey's daily gobbling occurs from his roost at dawn. Up there with his pink feet curled around a limb, a tom can ring a maximum amount of countryside to attract hens, while at the same time eyeballing danger approaching from afar.

In mountainous and hilly terrains, I find that Eastern turkeys prefer to roost just below knolls and points of ridges, and a third of the way to halfway down hillsides. In flatlands, Easterns will roost

Gobblers generally like to roost on high points of ground. They roar from their tree limbs at dawn to attract hens while scanning the woods below for potential danger. (Photo by Leonard Lee Rue III)

just about anywhere, but often high in a hardwood tree on a little hummock or atop a dry point in a swamp.

Good roosting sites are often few and far between in Rio Grande country, which helps you narrow down choice locations for morning hunts. I like to scout a ranch until I find the tallest cottonwood or live oak trees rimming a river or creek. On many trips to Texas, I've encountered 10 to 30 Rio gobblers packed into an oak roost along a waterway, bellowing to beat the band at dawn.

Merriam's turkeys travel around a lot in the spring, often roosting in ponderosa pines one night and sleeping in Gambel's oaks several miles away the next. The best way to keep tabs on the bearded vagabonds is to cover big chunks of country at dusk, locator calling to pinpoint the quarry for the next morning's hunt. In my experience, Merriam's and Rio Grandes love to gobble at dusk (unlike many Easterns and Osceolas), so putting one or more western toms to bed is generally no big deal.

Osceolas typically roost in moss-laden cypress swamps where alligators splash, birds shriek and bobcats prowl the misty predawn. To me, this adds yet more intrigue to the early-morning adventure.

But don't feel the panicky need to wade into a Florida blackwater swamp after your turkey. Set up near an adjacent ranch pasture or open burn, because that is where the dark-winged toms will likely fly down to strut for hens at dawn.

Locator Calling

A hunter who can boom out perfect barrel owl hoots with his natural voice and play a crow call like a flute sounds real pretty. I say more power to him, because he is all wrapped up in the spring obsession and hence perfecting his turkey-chasing technique. That said, I think that early-morning locator calling is one of the most overrated strategies in spring gobbler hunting.

Let me explain. With record numbers of mature toms inhabiting many areas today, one of them is apt to gobble on his own at dawn if we would just give him the chance. This rarely happens. Most hunters cannot wait to leap from their trucks and bring down the predawn woods with thunderous owl hoots and raucous crow battles.

To the contrary, try hitting the woods and laying low for a while. Let a roosted turkey do his thing. Some toms gobble early in the dark. Most roar at silvery daybreak. But a few wait until after gray shooting light to sound their love alerts.

A single-note hoot on an owl call is often all that is needed to shock a gobble from a hot tom roosted nearby. If a gobbler fails to bellow at your first hoot, scale up to moderately aggressive owling.

By waiting for a turkey to gobble on his own, you can make a silent and unobtrusive approach to him. This can give you a leg up when dueling skittish gobblers that have been hammered with hoots and crow calls by other hunters all spring. Since toms can recognize the distinct voices of live hens, and even key in to particular types of hunters' yelping, it only goes to reason that they can become call-shy to overly used locator calls.

Now don't get me wrong. Locator calling is an intricate part of the spring game, just not the panacea many hunters make it out to be. You must often locator call to shock responses from tight-lipped birds during the dreaded gobbling lull,

High-pitched coyote howling is great for shocking gobbles from long-range toms across the country. One April in Texas, Gary Roberson howled a gobble from this Rio Grande, which I then called in and killed.

(see Chapter 10). And during any phase of the spring season, commonsense locator calling can help you pinpoint roosted gobblers.

If a turkey fails to gobble on his own at dawn, don't get all excited and blast away on your owl hooter. Just float out a single-note hoot with a flutter on the end of it. If a hot turkey is roosted nearby, he will hammer the call. If no response, scale up to a moderately loud eight-note owl hoot.

Most hunters fail to pull out their crow calls until after gray light has seeped into the woods. I believe this is a mistake. Seems everywhere I hunt across the Eastern turkey's range, I hear crows cawing earlier and earlier each morning, often in the pitch-black predawn. If no turkeys are gobbling in an area, being the first raucous crow of the day can often elicit a response.

Probably the most effective but underutilized locator call going is the coyote howler. It is loud, sharp and high-pitched, excellent for shocking gobbles from distant birds.

I once hunted in Texas with my friend Gary Roberson, expert predator caller and owner of Burnham Brothers game calls. "Watch this," Gary would say before tooting his brass-colored coyote trumpet. And then Rio Grandes would gobble like crazy in all directions, as if suddenly poked with a cattle prod. One morning Gary howled a roaring gobble from a fine three-year-old longbeard, which I then yelped in and shot.

Later the same day, Roberson and I hooked up with a couple of friends who were hunting the opposite end of the ranch. "We heard you howling," said one of them, smiling. "It sounded great to us and even better to the turkeys. Every time you howled, they gobbled all around us."

Tooting his howler, Roberson had located gobblers two miles away! Enough said about the shocking power of coyote calls.

While you might expect Rio Grandes and Merriam's to respond to a coyote howler, the locator call can be effective in Eastern habitats as well. Remember, it is the shocking power of a locator device, not the actual sound of it, that causes turkeys to bellow. We have few coyotes where I hunt in Virginia (good news for our turkey flock), yet I've raised many gobblers with a brass trumpet that Gary Roberson gave me.

If you strike no early-morning gobblers with a locator call, turn to hen talk. Float out a couple of clucks and soft yelps, just in case a tight-lipped gobbler has flown down nearby. Scale up to moderately excited yelps and then to aggressive cutting, which to me is the ultimate gobbling stimulus and the most consistently effective locator call of all.

A.M. Setups

Okay, a roosted turkey roars, either on his own or in response to one of your locating devices. Move quickly 50 yards or so in his direction and check up, waiting for him to gobble again so you can pinpoint his location.

Drawing a precise line to a roosted gobbler is critical. Depending on the lay of the land and the stage of leaf growth on the deciduous trees, you can hear a turkey gobble from his limb a mile or more away.

Keep in mind that a turkey who gobbles facing directly away from you sounds more distant than he really is. If you creep too close

Listen for gobbler thunder from a strategic vantage at dawn. This allows you to hear distant gobbles clearly, and positions you above any turkey that roars close by. Upon hearing a faraway gobble, slip 50 yards or so in that direction and check up. Listen for the bird to bellow one or two more times so you can zero in on his precise location. Then use available cover and wrinkles in the terrain to slip as close as possible to a roosted gobbler before setting up to call.

without keeping tabs on a roosted turkey, either waiting for him to gobble on his own or checking him with a call, he may blow the hat off your head when he spins back around on his branch and roars in your face. It's easy to bump a bird that you thought was roosted 200 yards away but was really only 150 yards distant. Never try to slip in too tight unless you have pinpointed a gobbler's tree!

An excellent way to do this is to key into the drumming of toms. As mentioned in Chapter 1, a gobbler drums for the same reason that he gobbles—to lure hens. On calm mornings, I've heard the *pfft, duuummm* of turkeys in peak breeding mode more than 100 yards away.

Tuning into drumming allows you to draw lines on roosted toms who may not gobble much, but who will in all likelihood drum intensely. Many times I have slipped down misty ridges at dawn, listening for gobbles that never materialized, but jumping for joy when I heard an old bird drumming his subtle love tunes. The best thing about keying into drumming is that once you hear it, you know a gobbler is close. Start searching for a calling station.

All things considered, you should be able to slip within 200 yards of a roosted gobbler on most hunts. I prefer to hunt aggressively, using cover of darkness and ridges and hollows to sneak within 100 to 125 yards of a gobbler's tree whenever possible. I want to be breathing down an old warrior's neck when he flies down.

Years ago, the old-time turkey hunters could get by with setting up 300 to 400 yards away from roosted gobblers, and then soft-calling for hours and waiting for the love-starved toms to drift their way. No so today in most instances. Many of the toms you encounter will have hens and possibly jakes and subordinate two-year-old gobblers roosted nearby. All these turkeys create the ultimate calling competition for you.

By getting in tight on a roosted gobbler, you become a legitimate player in the early-morning ritual. Calling aggressively, you can often rile up the turkeys and pull them your way. If you fail to lure a dominant gobbler, you may draw a satellite longbeard into shotgun or bow range. An unexpected but welcome treat!

If you set up too far away at dawn, a gobbler roosted with hens will likely hit the ground and shun your calling. Why should he stroll over to check you out when he already has more mates than he can handle?

Also, if a turkey is roosting solo and gobbling hard, which is the dream scenario that we all pine for, you may be in for a major letdown if you set up too far away. The potential is there for a live hen to scoot in and intercept a gobbler working to your calls.

By setting up tight on a roosted gobbler, you become a legitimate player in the early-morning ritual. You can excite a tom with calling and perhaps pull him in before live hens appear on the scene.

I've heard and actually seen this happen many times over the years. In fact, just last April in Missouri, a turkey roared at my every cluck and yelp, hot and interested but taking his sweet time strutting in from 150 yards out. Suddenly I heard the unmistakable sound of turkey feet shuffling leaves to my left. Certain that a satellite tom was running in to my calls, I eased my gun barrel around, ready to take him when his white-capped head and dangling beard materialized.

I watched helplessly as an eight-pound hen raced past me at five yards, beelining for the old sultan who was playing my game. The gall of her! My turkey never gobbled again, didn't have to. His gobbling had attracted the hen, as nature designed it. Had I set up 50 yards tighter, the gobbler may have strutted into gun range before my sassy competition had the time to steal him.

An exception to the tight setup rule often comes when chasing Rio Grandes and Merriam's. On some western hunts, I've been able to use cover of darkness to slip within 100 yards of gobblers roosted in live oak, cottonwood or ponderosa pine trees. When the toms pitched down in the gray half-light, I yelped once or twice, then took 'em as they strutted in. Piece of cake.

Other times, however, when Rios or Merriam's were roosted in pockets of trees bordered by huge prairies or meadows (a common occurrence out West), I was forced to call from 400 yards or so away. To try to sneak across the open ground at dawn with multiple sets of keen eyes watching my every move would have been foolhardy, serving only to spook every gobbler out of the country.

Guess what? On every one of those long-range hunts, the gobblers flew down with hens and marched directly away from my setups. No need to come across a quarter-mile of open prairie to check me out.

40 YARDS

THE HIDDEN SETUP

Most toms hang up from your calling for one simple reason—they fail to see a yelping hen. Whenever possible, set up where a little ridge, ditch bank or similar rise in the terrain sits between you and a gobbling turkey. This way, when a gobbler tops the rise in search of a hidden, yelping hen, he is just about in shotgun range. Take the first good shot you have at an incoming turkey. Once a tom crests a rise but fails to see a hen, he will sense that something is amiss and quickly vacate the area.

Whenever you are forced to set up a country mile from western turkeys, or Easterns for that matter, call aggressively at dawn in hopes of getting a gobbler or two to pitch out in your direction. But if a spring flock does the ordinary and simply drops straight down from their trees and begins to drift away, move on the birds immediately to cut them off.

A man wise in the ways of western turkeys once told me, "Rios and Merriam's lace up their track shoes once they hit the ground each morning, high-stepping for a strutting zone or a watering hole. Yelping in unison, the 10 best turkey callers in the world couldn't turn 'em around." I have found that to be the case. So move quickly from distant setups, circling around and into their travel corridors before western toms end up miles away. Specific maneuvering strategies are found in Chapter 9.

If you are familiar with the turf you are hunting—a major advantage when working a roosted gobbler—always maneuver around the gray woods to take a fence, creek, gully or other turkey-hanging hazard out of play (more on this in the following chapter). And try to set where you can see only 35 to 50 yards in the direction of the limb-hanging bird.

Put a little rise in the terrain, say a ditch bank or the lip of a ridge, between you and a gobbling turkey. Remember, when a tom flies down to hook up with a hen, he will burn holes in the woods looking for her. If you are set up in a creek bottom, oak flat or other open area with thin understory, where a turkey can see 100 yards or so your way, he'll likely hang up because he fails to see a calling hen over there. But if you hide behind a little terrain wrinkle, he will often get impatient and crest the rise in search of the hen. And when he does, he is just about in shotgun range.

The Key Transition

Once set up, it is possible to become so enthralled with the mesmerizing gobbling of a roosted turkey that you miss the key transitional element of the morning. You never hear the tom leave his tree!

This is forgivable when a foxy bird slips silently from his limb, as some do. But most hard-gobbling turkeys flex and pump their wings and crash to the forest floor, sounding as if an elephant has fallen from the sky. Listen intently for swishing or thundering wings, as they offer invaluable clues as to what is unfolding before you.

Did just the gobbler fly down? If so, you have no calling competition. But if you hear several turkeys stagger from their limbs, hens were likely roosted nearby. You must call more aggressively.

On the bright side, a flurry of wings might indicate that a subordinate longbeard or two was roosted alongside the gobbling turkey. Be ready for a silent tom to slip into your calls.

Many gobblers you work on the roost will pitch straight down at first light, revealing little. But if a tom sails away from your initial tree clucks or yelps, this likely means: (1) he's leery of calling; or (2) you're set up in a place where he feels uncomfortable traveling. You may have to tone down your calling or switch calls. And you might be better off maneuvering quickly to cut him off.

If your tree yelping piques a gobbler's interest, he may sail off his limb toward you. This is exciting and offers a major tactical advantage. Key into the gobbler's thrashing wings, and the instant he crashes down, slowly twist your body and level your shotgun in his direction. He'll never notice the slight movement as he gathers himself from flying down.

The sharpest old sultan might glide over your head before touching down, planning to circle in to your calls from behind. If you see a turkey pulling this slick aerial maneuver, freeze. In mid-flight, he's looking down for the calling hen. The moment you hear him crash land behind you, swivel quickly around your setup tree, primed for his sneaky approach.

Calling Solo Gobblers

Over-calling to spring gobblers on the roost. Without question, the biggest mistake turkey hunters make! Most of the time, too much yelping at dawn hangs a tom on his limb as he waits to see you, the hot-to-trot hen, walk under his tree.

Also, heated calling can keep a turkey gobbling his heart out. Thrilling to hear, but not something you want. There is a grave risk that he will gobble up live hens or other hunters, hence ruining an otherwise golden opportunity.

Read a turkey's gobbling and drumming to determine if and how much to call to him in the tree. If a bird is roaring love tunes and you hear no hens talking, don't call to him too early. I know, I know, this is tough to do! But wait until you think it is just about time for the old devil to pitch down, then utter a soft tree cluck or yelp just to let him know you're there.

If he honors your sweet talk with a rattling gobble, shut the heck up. The gobbler is hot and anxious and knows precisely where you are. But if he fails to respond, cluck and yelp a little louder to focus his attention your way.

Once a solo gobbler pitches from his tree, hit him with a fly-down cackle and whip your wing for added realism. If the turkey gobbles hard and moves your way, you might not need to call again.

If he still doesn't gobble at you a second time, that is all right. Let him fly down before calling again. Once the turkey hits the dirt, give him time to settle his feathers and then hammer him with a fly-down hen cackle, whipping a turkey wing for added realism.

If the turkey gobbles hard at you and moves your way, you might not need to call again. Give him time to work, for he is playing the game! If he hangs up after five minutes or so, toss him some soft clucks, yelps and purrs. If still no gobbler is in gun or bow range, scale up to moderately aggressive yelping.

Try this calling scheme one morning. If it doesn't work, reverse strategy the next day. Wait for a solo tom to fly down, then back up your fly-down cackle with spirited yelping and cutting.

Remember, every wild turkey that roams this earth is uncannily unpredictable. Some respond best to soft calling, while others trip over their beards running to loud, animated yelping. Vary your calling schemes but remember this: All toms will likely hang on their limbs and gobble like crazy—and so doing minimize your odds of success—if you call too much before their big, red feet touch the ground.

Calling Gobblers With Hens

Shivering with excitement, you set up near a turkey ringing the dawn with nature's ultimate mating call. Then your heart sinks as you detect the dreaded tree clucking of hens.

With record numbers of hens encircling record numbers of gobblers today, this is a frustrating but common dilemma. Still, lowering the boom on a henned-up longbeard is doable if you key into the
following strategies.

For starters, the odds soar in your favor when you hunt familiar
ground and pattern the daily movements of a gobbler with ladies. Listen to the turkeys fly down at least two mornings in a row, and a draw
a line to where they go. At dawn the next morning, set up in or near the
spring flock's travel corridor, the ultimate place to call in a longbeard.

PLAY THE GOBBLER'S MACHO GAME

*If you encounter several hens roosted to one side of a gobbler's tree, try this
trick. Make a wide circle through the predawn woods and set up opposite the
hens, which puts the roosted gobbler between you and your calling competition.
A breeding tom is a male chauvinist who may actually fly down away from
his ladies and strut gaudily for them first thing in the morning. If a macho
gobbler pitches out in your direction, you'll be the first hen on the scene. Use
a little soft calling to reel him in.*

Whether hunting familiar or virgin turf, it is sometimes impossible to determine where a henned-up and unpredictable old gobbler will go when he hits the ground. Heck, most turkeys don't even know where they want to go many mornings!

In this case, set up within 100 yards of a spring flock and pour the coals to your calling. This is the time to over-call to a gobbler in the tree. It takes lots of excited clucking and yelping to say, "Don't forget me, old boy, I'm over here too." Use your fly-down cackle call before his hens hit the ground and then really get with the calling to get a gobbler thinking your way.

Most hunters assume that every tom that roosts with hens pitches straight down to his ladies in the morning. This is often the case, but remember, a breeding gobbler is a notorious male chauvinist. I have encountered some cocky birds who actually fly down away from their hens and strut and drum love tunes in the ultimate display of dominance.

Use a gobbler's machismo to your advantage. If you hear hens tree yelping and clucking off to one side of a roosted tom, move swiftly to the opposite side of the gobbler's roost. Slip in tight and set up, but this time don't call to the bird while he is still in the tree. Wait to see if he flies down to your side. If so, let him revel in all his

If a gobbler flies down with hens and drifts away, remain seated and call sparingly for an hour or so. If his hens desert him to lay eggs, the stood-up gobbler might circle back to check you out. (Photo courtesy Perfection Turkey Calls)

gaudy splendor for a minute, then cluck and yelp softly. You'll be the nearest available hen, and the tom might strut over for a look.

If a gobbler and his hens pitch down, get together and drift away from your setup, a disappointing but likely occurrence, remain seated and continue calling for an hour or so. A gobbler might get tired of chasing the hens if they are unreceptive, or the ladies may leave him early to lay eggs. A stood-up gobbler will remember where you are, and he just might circle back to check you out.

I am constantly amazed at how many turkey hunters don't have the patience and mental stamina to play mind games with an old gobbler with hens. I know I move much too quickly on most hunts. It is a shame, really. Good things come to those who wait—in this case toms with beards dragging the ground.

Poor-Weather Tactics

Every hunter yearns for calm spring mornings when turkeys gobble like crazy on their limbs. But wrapped around those prime dawns are many windy and rainy days. To be successful over the long haul of a spring season, you must key poor-weather tactics into your battle plan.

I hate hunting in the wind, the bane of turkey hunters. But I go when the breeze bends the treetops, and here are some strategies that work for me.

On howling nights, I anticipate turkeys to roost near the bases of mountains and ridges, on the sides of canyons or in the bottoms of hollows—anywhere the terrain breaks the wind. Look for gobblers in trees with sturdy horizontal branches, where the birds are not whipped from side to side all night.

The wind often lies at dawn, so hunt early and aggressively. Move in tight on a gobbling turkey and call more spiritedly than normal while he is in the tree. Try to dupe a gobbler as soon as he hits the ground, because a half-hour or so after sunrise the wind typically gathers steam, limiting your hearing and the range of your calling.

Cover lots of country on breezy mornings, when toms may not gobble much if at all on their own. Maneuver upwind of where you anticipate toms to be roosted or strutting, and let your loud locator calls and hen cuts float downwind to the turkeys.

If you hear a wind-muffled gobble, set up quickly. The gobbler is likely closer than he sounds. And on breezy days, a tom may be ultra-spooky because his hearing is impaired. He may race to your calls, seeking the security of other turkeys.

Hunting in a steady downpour is uncomfortable and unproductive. Toms remain on their roosts late in the morning and do not gobble all that much.

That said, slipping back into a warm bed when rain pounds the roof is a terrible mistake. Many spring rains are merely showers or thunderstorms. Roll out of the sack, drive to a hunting area and wait in your truck. If and when the rain stops, gobblers will hammer away.

Upon flying down on nasty mornings, turkeys often flock to a nearby pasture, meadow or crop field. I think the birds hate to rub their feathers against wet saplings and understory in the woods—they feel better out in the open, where their heavy, oily feathers turn water like a Barbour coat. Also, rainy, dripping forests are loud, negating the birds' keen sense of hearing. No doubt turkeys feel safe in open spaces where they can see danger approaching from afar.

So check nearby fields, burns, prairie edges and the like for feeding hens and strutting gobblers on rainy mornings. A section in the following chapter is devoted to hunting and calling "field turkeys."

I find that toms often gobble like crazy on foggy, drizzly mornings. Check fields for feeding hens and strutting gobblers on rainy days.

Foggy, humid mornings may look and feel nasty, but they are prime times to hunt. I find that turkeys often gobble as hard or harder on misty mornings as they do on sparkling-clear days. I have yet to run across a wild turkey with a barometer hanging in his roost tree. An old sultan ripe with the rut will rattle away on both high- and low-pressure days.

A gray-haired Virginia hunter with who-knows-how-many coffee cans chock full of beards and spurs once told me, "Boy, you worry about the weather too much. The best mornin' to turkey hunt is the one when you can get off work!" That is just about right. Rain, wind or shine, get out there and engage a gobbler at dawn. It is the essence of spring turkey hunting.

It doesn't get any better than this—back at camp by 7:00 a.m. with an old Eastern longbeard and a hot cup of coffee.

While working a tom roaring from his limb at dawn might be the essence of spring hunting, calling in the sunny midday woods is often the best way to bag a gobbler like this 24-pound Iowa beauty.

Chapter 7

Midday Toms

It had been one heck of a morning in the creek bottom near the tiny town of Red Lick, Mississippi. My friend Will Primos, his video cameraman and I were guests on a private lease nestled amid some of the finest Eastern turkey country you could ever imagine. Gobblers were there in good numbers. Boy, were they ever.

We had two old toms roaring 120 yards from our setup trees at dawn. The plan was simple—we would pull a slick double team. While Will and the camera guy set up behind me and called "way too much and way too loud," as Primos often puts it, I would kill the biggest of the two birds during a scintillating hunt to be featured on an upcoming Primos video. No problem I thought as the first long-bearded sultan strutted magnificently into gun range.

At 35 yards I clucked on a diaphragm call. When the turkey dropped his tail feathers and craned his red periscope my way, I confidently pressed the shotgun's trigger—and missed clean as a whistle! Frustrating and embarrassing and on videotape for all the turkey hunting world to see.

But I wasn't done yet.

At the roar of my shotgun, a third turkey gobbled 100 yards below us in the creek bottom. "Let's see what he'll do," Primos whispered. We yelped excitedly in unison. The turkey rattled the foliage with a booming double gobble and moved in our direction! We fled frantically for setup trees.

Can you believe this old bird strutted within 20 yards and I didn't kill him either? I was set up in a terrible spot, which often happens when a turkey bellows close and causes you to dive for the nearest cover. And tentative from my earlier miss—I could not bear the pain and humiliation of missing two longbeards in 20 minutes on film—I was going to make sure of things before I pressed the trigger this time.

Lo and behold, the gobbler strutted in to my left, coming through a thick pocket of brush where turkeys are not supposed to come but often do. Before I knew it, the old devil had slipped between Primos and me where a safe shot was impossible. The cameraman captured the majestic Eastern with an 11-inch rope drumming and gobbling on film at 10 yards before he finally walked off to find another hen.

Now I am used to trials and tribulations in turkey hunting, but this was going too far. I knew the only way to save face and sanity was to pick up my head, and you can bet it was hanging mighty low at that point, and keep on hunting. Fortunately in Mississippi, you can call turkeys all day in the spring, so I left Primos and the cameraman after lunch and skulked off to find another gobbler.

Sitting on a ridge with ivory sunshine streaming through the oak trees, I cutt loudly on a slate call. I waited 10 minutes and called again. Around 1:00 p.m., the fourth gobbler of the day hammered my cutts! I sneaked 30 yards down the ridge and called again. The turkey roared 50 yards closer.

Minutes later I spied a ball of blue-red flame bobbing in the green foliage. I leveled my Remington on the turkey's head and neck, took a deep breath, said a little prayer and pressed the trigger. You could have heard my war whoop five miles away as I raced out to claim my sharp-spurred prize.

An unbelievable hunt? Not really. If you turkey hunt long enough, you are going to miss and mess up. You are also going to kill gobblers if you persevere and hunt in the middle of the day.

Combined, more than 25 Southeastern, Midwestern and Western states permit all-day spring gobbler hunting. I have visited many of these states over the years, and have lured in longbeards as late as 4:00 p.m. in March, April and May. Hunting all day is effective throughout the season. And even if you live in a state that requires you to beat feet out of the woods at 12:00 or 1:00 p.m., you can have a ball working your quarry from 9:00 in the morning until quitting time.

In fact, flipping through the pages of my turkey hunting journal, I find that 60 percent of the gobblers I have fooled in recent years hit the ground flopping between 9:00 a.m. and 4:00 p.m. I keep in close contact with many of the top turkey hunters in the country, and they report similar midday success.

While working an old monarch roaring from his limb in the misty dawn is the essence of spring hunting, slipping around and calling in sun-glistening fields, woods and prairies just might be your best chance to fill your gobbler tags. Here's how to set a strategic midday game plan into motion.

Locating Daytime Gobblers

As mentioned in the previous chapter, peak gobbling activity occurs at dawn, when toms call from their roosts to attract hens. After flying down, they strut, drum and gobble from convenient places to gather as many ladies as possible. When hens meet gobblers, the woods often fall as silent as a mausoleum as the turkeys

mix and mingle and do their thing. This early-morning lull is a tough time to hunt.

But along about 9:00 a.m., some hens begin to leave the gobblers, simply losing interest in them or slipping away to lay eggs. Lonesome toms driven by an uncontrollable urge to mate begin searching for more company.

To accomplish this, some hot two-year-old toms gobble like crazy on their own. Other turkeys, especially the old longbeards, strut and drum intensely, but may not gobble all that much. Ah, but you crank them up by covering lots of ground and locator calling effectively.

Use a crow call to locate gobblers strutting their tail feathers off at midday. Try to make a tom gobble at your caws two or three times so you can pinpoint his location before setting up to call.

Beginning in midmorning, walk old logging roads, field edges, ridges, power line rights-of-way, foot trails and similar terrain breaks that allow you to maneuver swiftly and quietly over miles of ground. Pause on ridges, knolls and other high vantages to listen for lonely toms gobbling on their own. If you listen from points too low, you might not hear a tom who gobbles only 200 yards away down in a hollow, just over the lip of a ridge or in a pocket of dense foliage. Turkeys on the ground can be difficult to hear, especially if they're facing away from you when they gobble.

To strike gobblers as you go, crow call aggressively from your listening posts. Try coyote howls or yips. And don't put away that reed-style owl hooter just yet. Barred owls are nocturnal birds that call most frequently at dawn and dusk, but I've had many gobblers bellow at owl hoots in midmorning and early afternoon.

To locate midday gobblers, simple clucking and yelping normally won't cut it. You need hen calls with more shocking power. I like to toss out a couple of moderately loud, excited yelps in hopes of striking an unseen tom strutting 100 to 200 yards away. Hearing nothing, I scale up to sharp cutting to shock gobbles from distant turkeys.

When you pull a single gobble from a midday turkey, your first instinct is to tear down the woods racing to him. Years ago, that was the thing to do. That bird was probably the only game in town, and you needed to get on him as fast as possible. But today, with record numbers of turkeys per square mile, lay back and try to make the turkey gobble a second and third time.

Clucking and yelping normally won't cut it at midday. Try locating strutting gobblers with short, sharp bursts of cutting on a friction call.

Give him another shot of the locator calling or hen yelping that he honored the first time. If he doesn't answer, move 50 to 100 yards in his direction and hammer him again.

If he still doesn't talk and you have lots of hunting ground left to cover, leave him alone. The turkey is not hot, and chances are he gave you only a cursory gobble as he strutted amid a bevy of hens. You're better off leaving the old warrior to have his fun and moving along in hopes of striking a lonely bird.

Midday Setups

When you raise a gobbler, proceed quickly but with caution. Turkeys on the ground are ultra-spooky, constantly scanning the woods, fields and prairies for lurking predators. And since they often gobble infrequently, it is difficult to pinpoint their location.

Creep along and blow a crow call in hopes a gobbler will respond one or two more times so you can draw a precise line on him. You should be able to maneuver within 150 to 200 yards of strutting gobblers on most hunts. And since you can see and read the contours of terrain in the middle of the day, you can often slip much closer by using ridges, hollows, creek beds and other terrain features to cover your movements.

When you sense it is time to begin searching for a calling position, try to anticipate where the gobbling turkey will end up for the day. If he is not already set up in a strut zone—a secluded, fairly open place where he feels safe and comfortable attracting hens and keeping a sharp eye out for potential danger—there's a good bet he will move that way soon.

I find that Eastern gobblers love to strut atop ridges, knolls and bluffs, and in open creek bottoms, oak flats, fields and burns. Western gobblers typically establish display zones in mountain meadows, canyon bottoms and short-grass plains with good visibility.

If you can read the country and set up between a gobbling turkey and his potential strut zone, you create the perfect scenario for a daytime ambush. The gobbler already wants to move in that direction. Your sweet hen talk floating from somewhere along the old boy's line of travel can cause him to zoom in.

Fixing to set up, scan the terrain for any barrier that can hang up an approaching turkey. Most of the time, a tom is reluctant to cross a fence, creek, river, ditch, gully, strip of thick brush or similar hazard. Remember, he wants you to come to him. And even if he decides to make the first more, it will likely be along a safe and convenient strutting route.

I've had a few lovesick desperadoes fly rivers, hop ditches and burrow through brush like rabbits to come to my calls. While these hunts certainly made me feel good about my calling skills, they were nothing more than freak exceptions to the rule. If you expect to lure toms consistently, circle around and take even the tiniest hazard out of play before setting up to yelp.

From Texas to Alabama to Florida to South Dakota, you may encounter a midday turkey roaring near an old ranch road or logging two-track. If so, try a roadside setup.

If a gobbler roars at your cutts from across a creek, go after him if you can. Nine times out of 10 you have to get on the same side of water with a turkey to call him in.

LOGGING ROAD SETUP

Whenever possible, set up to call a gobbling turkey near a bend in an old logging road. When a tom steps out into a curve to strut and look both ways down the road for hens, you can lower the boom on him.

Old roads, especially those closed to vehicles, draw wild turkeys like magnets in the spring. Hens peck for green shoots and insects and dust in old road beds. Toms love to strut up and down the woodland alleys in search of feeding and preening ladies.

If you set up to call facing a long, straight stretch of a turkey highway, your odds of luring a tom are 50-50 in my experience. A red-hot gobbler may parade 100 yards or more down a woodland corridor to investigate your yelping, but a wary old longbeard will likely slam on the brakes 70 yards or so out and wait for the hen to cruise to him.

To minimize hangups, set up 20 yards off a road bed, amid foliage and against a tree but still with a good view of the two- track. Scratch leaves as you call softly and seductively. By mimicking a hen

Old logging roads are turkey highways. Calling from a roadside setup is a good way to lure a tom searching for hens that feed in the woods' opening. (Photo courtesy Perfection Turkey Calls)

feeding or nesting just out of sight in nearby cover, you can often reel a reluctant gobbler down a road and into your lap.

Here's another trick. Whenever possible, set up within shotgun range of a curve in a farm or logging road. A strutting gobbler often steps out of the woods and into a road bend, where he can attract hens from either direction. From a curve setup, you can nail a crafty tom who pulls this slick maneuver.

Finally, regardless of where you set up, choose a midday calling position in the shade. Mottled shadows in the sunlit woods enhance the effectiveness of your camouflage.

The Call-Patterning Technique

What I refer to as "call patterning" is effective on gobblers anywhere and any time of the day or season. I find the technique to be particularly dynamite for cranking up and luring midday toms.

Call patterning, which involves feeling out a gobbler with a full range of passive to aggressive hen talk, is like toying with a car radio. Just as you run the dial from classical to country to rock, lowering or intensifying the volume, you vary your turkey calling. Just as you strive to find music that pleases your ear, you hope to strike a magical chord that will bring a longbeard running.

Having set up strategically on a daytime turkey, pull your favorite diaphragm, box, slate or tube call from your vest. Which device you use is academic. The key is to use it diversely.

Your patterning technique should center around your personal style of turkey calling. If you feel most comfortable and confident clucking, yelping, and purring softly and sparingly, begin a midday gobbler with passive calling. If you are an aggressive caller, as I generally am, start a turkey with sharp, moderately loud series of clucks, yelps and cuts.

Then listen and read the gobbler's response. If he roars and moves toward you, give him more of the same and then shut up to give the turkey time to work. But if he fails to respond or gobbles awhile but then hangs up, begin a full range of call patterning.

Depending on your style, this involves either raising or lowering the volume and intensity of your yelping. If you've started a gobbler with soft, subtle calling, scale up to moderately excited yelping. Continue to read the gobbler. Still failing to strike the chord, turn it up another notch, yelping loudly and cutting sharply, hoping to jump-start the turkey.

Call-patterning, running a full range of passive to aggressive yelping, can be a deadly tactic on midday gobblers.

If aggressive calling has failed to produce, tone down. Try a series of fast but low-intensity yelps. If still no favorable response, scale down to clucks and yelps, bottoming out with soft, subtle clucks and purrs.

A key here: Your call patterning must sound authentic. While a live hen readily varies the volume and intensity of her yelping, she isn't an extremist. She won't cluck softly, then back it up with loud, sharp cutting. Conversely, rarely will an aggressively cutting hen suddenly turn to faint yelping. It isn't natural, as hens do not change their moods that quickly.

But live hens do call pattern up and down, running a full range of octaves as they sweet-talk gobblers. Do the same and sooner or later you should strike those magical notes that bring a midday tom on the run.

Field Turkey Tactics

Through my compact binocular, I examined the old gobbler strutting in the Georgia meadow and immediately coined him "The Emperor". My, he was a magnificent if gaudy sight, certainly the ruler of his domain! As the turkey popped his wings and vibrated his fan and twirled in circles, the April sunshine weaved a rainbow of colors on his ebony breast feathers. Beneath a white- crowned head and cherry red neck, The Emperor's beard swept the clover.

The gobbler turned his huge fan to me, and I ducked into the hardwoods rimming the field. When he twirled back my way, I froze. I inched along and slipped within 150 yards of the royal turkey.

For an hour that old boy honored my yelps and clucks with violent gobbling and explosive strutting sure to suppress every peasant tom in the vicinity. Several times his majesty marched within 80 yards of my setup, and I was confident he was coming.

Suddenly he broke strut, walked to the opposite side of the field and ducked into a thicket a half-mile away. The Emperor had not been spooked, he was just being a "field turkey," wonderfully skittish and unpredictable.

Regardless of where and which subspecies of wild turkey you hunt, you will encounter gobblers strutting in wide-open spaces. Easterns spinning in green fields or young clearcuts and burns with low-growing vegetation. Merriam's displaying their blond-tipped tails in mountain meadows and short-grass plains. Rio Grandes all puffed up on dry, rocky prairies scattered throughout the Texas brush.

Hens feed and gobblers strut in fields, clearcuts, burns and meadows in the middle of the day. Hunting sharp-eyed toms in the wide-open spaces is a supreme challenge.

I refer to these birds collectively as field turkeys and feel the need to devote a section to hunting and calling them. You see, dueling gobblers strutting their stuff in open terrains is one of the most common—and difficult—scenarios in the midday pursuit.

Wild turkeys love to visit greening fields, meadows and other open habitats on spring days. Hens gather there to glean tender plants and nab grasshoppers and other insects. After feeding, the ladies often nest in the brushy edges of fields or in nearby thickets or cutovers.

Gobblers come to open spaces to see and be seen. Toms set up in or near the middle of fields, where they can strut royally to attract hens and eyeball predators approaching from afar. A sharp-eyed gobbler's ability to scan 360 degrees of open turf is what makes hunting him so tough.

As you prospect for turkeys at midday, approach open areas with extreme caution. Sneak slowly in the surrounding timber or brush and use ridges, hollows and other wrinkles in the terrain to conceal your every move. Make a sudden, ill-timed maneuver in a sliver of an opening, and you'll send a field gobbler and his hens skittering away like baitfish darting from a hungry bass.

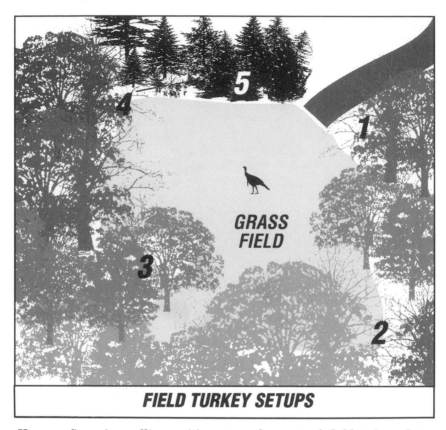

FIELD TURKEY SETUPS

Here are five prime calling positions to employ on tough field turkeys. Setup 1 is good because a gobbler will often strut in a farm or logging road that spills into a green field or meadow. Turkeys often enter and leave an open area through corners; setups 2 and 4 might put you in their travel lane. Any point that juts out into field (3) offers good visibility and is a hot spot to yelp from. Position 5 could be great on a rainy morning when a gobbler might be roosted in nearby pines — he might sail from his evergreen limb and alight in the field, or pitch down and walk past your setup en route to his strutting area.

If possible, gain a hidden and strategic vantage and glass a field, meadow, prairie strip or other open area with your compact binocular. If the turf appears to be devoid of birds, try to raise a gobbler that might be strutting behind a little rise or bend in a field or back in a nearby fringe of timber.

Toss out a raucous crow call or an owl hoot. If you get no response, cutt aggressively on a diaphragm, box or slate call.

If a turkey gobbles out in a field or along its perimeter, dive for cover. He is probably a lot closer than he sounds, as the acoustics of open areas deaden the roar and rattling quality of a tom's gobble. Also, if a gobbler is close and sans hens, he may be fixing to run you over.

When a field turkey gobbles 100 yards or more away but fails to move in your direction, he is likely set up in a comfortable strut zone. Be patient and continue to glass. You may eventually see the gobbler parading up and down his strut corridor.

At this point, try hammering him with aggressive calling. If you see him make the slightest effort to move your way, tone down. If he hangs up, pour more calling to him in hopes of making him break strut and zoom your way.

Most field turkeys are loathe to leave their strut zones, which means you must go to them. Glass a bird and wait until he swings to the far end of his zone with his fan toward you, then sneak slowly, using the bordering woods and any wrinkle in the terrain to conceal your approach.

If possible, slip within 100 yards of the front edge of a gobbler's strut zone and look quickly for a place to set up. Keep in mind that turkeys often travel near the heads and corners of fields and along any points that jut out into the middle. Field corners and points with adequate cover are prime calling stations.

Again, consider setting up near an old logging or ranch road leading into a field. As mentioned earlier, two-tracks are natural travel lanes for turkeys. I've called in and killed several Eastern and Rio Grande gobblers strutting down road beds that spilled into meadows and prairies.

Regardless of where you locate, try to avoid calling from right on the edge of a field. A turkey might see you, or more likely he will see that no hen is over there. Why should he risk strutting over for a look?

Ideal is to set up 15 yards or so deep in cover that rims an open area. Put enough trees or brush between you and a field gobbler, and he might think a hen is playing hard to get back in there. Eventually a tom with no company may get impatient and sneak over for a peek.

When choosing a calling site, stay well hidden in the shade, but locate where you can see a field turkey at all times. The nice thing about eyeballing a strutting gobbler is that he indicates when you need to call and when you don't.

Your natural tendency is to yelp hard to a gobbler you see spinning out in the open spaces. But the more you call, the more he is apt to stay in one spot and strut. Just let the turkey know you're there

OPEN FIELD

IF GOBBLER STRUTS TOWARD DECOY, HE'LL PASS BY YOUR SETUP

SET DECOY 20 YARDS PAST SETUP

DECOY TRICK

Try placing a foam decoy 20 yards past your setup tree. Many old gobblers like to strut in and stop 20 to 30 yards away from a decoy, waiting for the hen to make the final move to them. A gobbler who hangs up from a decoy staked beyond your setup might hang up right where you want him—in front of your shotgun barrel. Always place a turkey decoy in an open area where you can see and ward off a reckless nitwit who might resort to stalking your fake.

by tossing him a few soft clucks, yelps and purrs. And give him time, perhaps an hour or more, to come to you.

What if passive calling fails to produce? Sometimes challenging a field turkey with gobbling and aggravated purring can change his mind from strutting for hens to kicking your butt. Watch the gobbler, for you can tell quickly whether or not he likes your aggressive calls. If he shows no response or moves away, shut up before you spook him out of the field. But if your gobbles and purrs rile him up and cause him to look or move your way, pour it on and he may come to honor your challenge.

Try aggressive hen calling if a field gobbler has ladies, a distinct possibility. Yelp and cutt loudly and sharply, hoping to excite the hens and pull them your way with his majesty in tow. This is admittedly a long-shot tactic, but it has worked for me a couple of times.

If a turkey simply won't respond to your calls, wait for him to strut behind a rise in the field or turn a corner and move out of sight. Then crawl out into the field and stake a fake hen within 30 yards of your setup (if decoys are legal in the area you are hunting).

Used in conjunction with soft or aggressive hen calling, a foam decoy spinning around in the breeze can be deadly on a field turkey. When a gobbler returns to the near edge of his strut zone and spots a potential mate that he believes has just stepped out of the cover, he may race over to check her out.

In Illinois one spring, a field turkey ran former world champion caller Steve Stoltz and I around in circles for a couple of hours. During a break in the heated battle, my friend pulled a foam decoy from his vest and offered this tip.

I am not a huge fan of turkey decoys, but I often use them on a field gobbler. When a strutting tom spies a foam hen that he thinks has just stepped out of the cover and into a field, he will sometimes zoom over to check her out.

Midday calling is a hot tactic on public land. Once a legion of hunters leaves an hour or so after dawn, you'll have the sunlit woods to yourself as you prospect for strutting longbeards. That's how Harold Knight (left), David Hale (right) and I bagged these big Kentucky gobblers.

"Don't set your decoy directly in front of you, but 20 or 30 yards beyond your setup," Stoltz said. "This puts you between the decoy and the strutting gobbler. A field turkey is tough—he wants to come in 50 or 60 yards and wait for the hen to come the rest of the way. By placing a decoy beyond you, the gobbler will often strut within shotgun or bow range on his final approach."

That Illinois gobbler shunned our decoy and whipped our butts, but I have since used Stoltz's tip to lure a couple of toms those final few yards. It is just another little twist that can pay off big time when hunting tough field turkeys.

Midday: Prime Time For Public-Land Hunts

Midday hunting is time consuming. You'll have to take off work or go in late. But remember, 95 percent of the other turkey hunters must leave for work by 7:30 a.m. or so. You'll likely have the woods to yourself during midmorning and afternoon hunts.

This is what makes midday hunting so effective on public lands. Once the hoards of hunters leave for home, camp or work, you can set out to strike and work gobblers.

Most every spring I hunt in Iowa and Missouri with M.A.D. call maker and video producer Mark Drury. Over the years, we have hunted some of the finest private ground in America, pristine hardwood ridges and flats teeming with 25-pound Eastern gobblers that seem intent on bringing down the woods with violent gobbling each morning. So it always amazes me when after a morning of working but failing to kill a turkey on private land, Drury says, "Hop in the truck, let's head for a public area."

"You've got to be kidding," I generally respond. What turkey hunter in his right mind would pass up the chance to hunt private Midwestern ground during the prime midmorning hours in favor of a heavily hunted public area?

"The gobblers are there," Drury says and away we go.

Often there is a truck or two parked in the public areas, but by far most of the early-morning turkey chasers are long gone. It amazes me to this day how many gobblers we locate by driving around back roads and cutting aggressively on friction calls. We normally strike turkeys from half the places we stop. We chase public-land gobblers right up until quitting time at 1:00 p.m.! I feel confident you can do the same.

Midday turkey hunting is about perseverance. After missing a gobbler one morning in Mississippi, I cutt up this longbeard at 1:00 p.m. Toting him from the woods saved the day!

The Final Word

Midday turkey hunting is all about perseverance. It is hard to go all day when you have been up since 4:00 a.m, the sun is sizzling, the temperature hovers in the 80s or 90s and the snakes and insects are active. But remember, somewhere out there is a lonely gobbler waiting to roar at your spirited crow calls or aggressive hen cutts. And if you missed a turkey or messed up or both first thing that morning, as I did on that Mississippi hunt years ago, I can assure you that toting out a midday gobbler will be sweet salvation.

By casting your calling, bouncing yelps left and right off the palm of your hand, you mimic a hen moving around in the woods. This adds realism to your calling and keeps a gobbler guessing where you are.

Chapter 8

Advanced Turkey Talk

I popped the lid of my box call, clucking sharply. The gobbler raced down the ridge line, skidded to a halt 75 yards away, fanned into brilliant, sun-drenched strut, boomed a double gobble and marched back up the mountainside.

"Trying to lead this hen uphill, huh?" I reasoned. So I obliged, slipping off the ridge, falling into a deep hollow, circling wide, climbing the backside of the mountain and topping out above the turkey 15 minutes later.

I raspy-yelped on a diaphragm. *Gaaaarrrraoobbbble.* I expected the turkey to be strutting near the top of the ridge, but not 60 yards away! Diving for cover, I heard the bird running in the leaves and twisted around to level my shotgun down the slope. With the beard-swinging gobbler at 18 steps and closing fast, I pulled the Remington's trigger in self-defense.

Mountain turkey hunting is an intriguing chess game of tactical maneuvers—the most important of which is *to set up and call ridge-running gobblers from above.* Sitting downhill from that old Appalachian gobbler, I had called for over an hour. The turkey gobbled and drummed at my every cluck, yelp and cutt, yet simply would not commit down the ridge.

Why? Because descending even the gentlest slope, it is tough for a turkey to turn and run back uphill if he encounters a fox, bobcat, coyote, or other predator. A toms feels safe strutting, gobbling and drumming from a knoll, ridgetop or similar vantage, trying to call a hen up to a spot where he can see very well. A hot-to-trot gobbler will, however, sometimes walk, strut or even run uphill to hen talk. He senses he can easily swap ends and run or glide off a mountainside if danger approaches.

Whether you hunt Eastern turkeys amid rolling, 700-foot-high ridges or Merriam's in 8,000-foot mountains, always try to maneuver

around and call to gobblers from above or least from the same eleva-
tional plane. "Topping out" will greatly improve your success.

That is just one of 25 turkey calling tips to be found in the following pages. To help you score more beards and spurs, I have keyed
this potpourri of advanced techniques and little tricks to common
situations you are likely to encounter in the spring woods.

Cast Your Yelping

When a turkey hen moves around the spring woods, she is fidgety,
walking, pecking and scratching here and there, forever moving and

1,2,3 – PRIME CALLING STATIONS
4,5 – POOR CALLING SPOTS

TOPPING OUT FOR TURKEYS

*You should strive to hunt any type of game from above. Wild turkeys, which
feel most comfortable moving uphill to calling, are no exception. In this example, setups 1 and 2 above the turkey are hot. Calling from number 3, on the
same level as a strutting gobbler, is a good option. Positions 4 and 5 below
the tom would be unproductive on most hunts.*

turning as she clucks, purrs and yelps. Key off of this by casting your yelping, calling to either side and behind as well as out in front of you. This adds much realism to your calling schemes, and on the toughest gobblers can be the final convincer.

While often overlooked by hunters who sound like hens chained to trees, throwing your calling is easy to accomplish. When using a diaphragm, practice yelping out the sides of your mouth until you can cast your calls left and right. You can also cup your hand to your mouth and bounce calls off your palm, though this requires movement and must be considered when a gobbler is closing.

With a slate, box or tube, be sure a turkey is out of sight, then hold the call off to one side or directly behind you. Varying the volume of your calls also helps their ventriloquial effects.

On a severely hung-up gobbler, try backing off 20 to 40 yards, yelping as you go. Then move left, right or back a few more steps, casting your calling all the while before repositioning. The tom may read your "float calls" to mean that the hen is moving away, whereupon he might gobble and strut in to rekindle her interest.

Convince A Gobbler

Just because a turkey gobbles at your calls does not mean he will come to them. You must involve him in the mock breeding game, convince him you are a hot little hen worth investigating.

When a turkey gobbles hard at you, his mating call rattling and with that unnerving quality, he is likely burning with desire, and most any style of competent yelping may pull him in. It's those aloof, sporadically gobbling turkeys that take convincing.

Start a stubborn gobbler with loud, excited clucks and yelps, tossing in a sharp cackle or cutt for good measure. If the turkey gobbles back at you, yelp or cutt vigorously back at him the instant he finishes gobbling. Repeat this rapid-fire scenario of "cutting in" on a turkey's gobbling until he finally cuts in on your calls. At this point, the tom's gobbling should be more frequent and intense, which means he is involved and perhaps convinced enough to come check you out.

Yelp Like A Gobbler

Mimicking gobbler yelps is an overlooked but often effective calling tactic. Gobbler yelping is dynamite if cold, rainy weather dictates a late spring in your hunt zone. Though the turkey break-up has begun, many gobblers will still be loosely congregated in winter flocks. Toms may become separated or just want male companionship, so they'll come to gobbler yelps.

Also, with record numbers of toms inhabiting many regions today, gobbler yelping can be effective all spring. You sound like a new tom in the social order, and other subdominant gobblers may seek you out. Gobbler yelping can also be excellent for challenging dominant toms with hens.

How do you yelp like a gobbler? I find it easiest to do on a multi-reed mouth diaphragm, or working in the low-pitched middle of a slate call. Whichever device you use, slow down the length and rhythm of your calls. A gobbler's yelps may be deep-throated and raspy or fairly clear, but they are always slower than hen yelps. Toss in deep-pitched gobbler clucks for added realism.

Smart Midday Locating

During midmorning or early afternoon, you cutt aggressively and raise a booming gobble. All fired up, you race toward the bird, yelping or cutting as you go to further pinpoint his location. You may be making a grave mistake!

Upon striking a midday gobbler, resist the urge of hen calling before you reach your setup. Remember, just as you are closing the distance to the turkey, he may be doing the same. The more you yelp and cutt, the faster he might come. If you and the gobbler blunder into one another, the jig is up.

Use a locator call to keep tabs on the gobblers you strike. A crow call is best, but an owl hooter or a hawk whistle can suffice. When a gobbler roars at your locator call within 150 yards, make your final approach, set up quickly and switch back to hen calling.

Calling Toms Across Hazards

When a creek, ditch, fence or other hazard hangs up a gobbler you're working, it's always best to maneuver around and take the obstacle out of play. But sometimes this is impossible. For example, a tom may strut on a bald knoll that overlooks a deep gully—try to skirt the obstacle or climb the ridge, and he'll see you. Or a bird might gobble his head off on the opposite side of a stream or river that is too deep to wade. On some hunts, you are forced into the unenviable position of trying to call a gobbler across a hazard.

Your best chance is to hit the turkey with a burst of loud, aggressive yelping and cutting, then lay down your calls for at least 20 minutes. The gobbler may walk back and forth along the obstacle, gobbling like crazy. After awhile, he might not be able to stand it. He may eventually walk or fly across the hazard to find that hot hen.

Your best chance of calling a reluctant gobbler across a hazard is to hit him with a burst of loud, aggressive yelping and cutting, then shut up for 20 minutes or longer. If the turkey is hot and alone, he may walk, hop or fly across to you. (Photo courtesy Perfection Turkey Calls)

The key is to pour on the calling, then shut up completely. If you call even one more time, the gobbler will likely stay put on the other side of the creek, ditch or fence, gobbling and strutting and waiting for you to come across to him.

Cackle To Swamp Gobblers

Turkeys that inhabit Southern swamps or bottomland forests laced with creeks, sloughs and backwaters cackle a lot. The birds utter these fast, excited calls not only when pitching up to or down from their roosts, but also when flying or hopping across water, which they naturally do many times each day.

Play off of this vocal tendency of the turkeys anytime you call in a water-logged habitat. Punctuating your clucks and yelps with fast, excited cackles is a realistic way to fire up and pull in an old dark-winged swamp gobbler.

Who's That Yawking?

Slipping through the woods and prospecting for turkeys, you suddenly detect the loud, coarse, slow-cadenced, one-to-three note

Jakes often travel with mature gobblers. If you hear a jake yawking, set up and yawk back to him on a raspy mouth diaphragm. He may come and bring a silent longbeard with him. (Photo courtesy Perfection Turkey Calls)

clucking or yelping of a jake. Set up and get ready, even if you fail to hear any gobbling nearby. One or more young gobblers that travel in a spring flock rarely gobble, but they often *yawk* each time a dominant tom struts for his hens.

Begin calling and mix in jake clucks and yelps of your own. I like to *yawk* slowly on a raspy mouth diaphragm. Try to lure the inquisitive young gobblers, who might bring with them an unexpected prize: A silent longbeard that you didn't know was strutting in the vicinity.

Point Your Box Or Slate

Do you hold your box call upright in the palm of your hand as you yelp or cutt excitedly to locate turkeys? If so, you are negating one of the box's major advantages: great volume. With the call's sound chamber pointed straight up, your yelps and cutts fade into thin air.

Cradle a box lightly in your palm, then turn your hand and the call perpendicular to the ground. Hold the box well away from your body, point its sounding chamber in the direction you want to cutt and pop the chalked handle fast and firmly against the sounding lip. This way, your cutts will penetrate a mile through a creek bottom, hollow or similar area where a gobbler may be strutting.

Hold a friction call away from your body and point it in the direction you want your yelps and cutts to flow. This maximizes the volume of your locator calls.

Use the same open stance when yelping or cutting on a slate call. Hold the cup (remember, up on your fingertips) and striker well away from your body. Face the call in the direction you want to yelp and cutt, and bear down hard on the peg for maximum volume.

Create A Big Fight

One April morning, I heard the brush-thrashing, wing-thumping, aggressive-purring fury of two gobblers fighting 100 yards away. I listened intently and determined that at least one subordinate tom paced the fringes of the war and shock gobbled sporadically. A couple of jakes *yawked* and half-gobbled. Somewhere in the vicinity a hen cutt aggressively.

Seems turkeys do respond to a fight like people do. A gobbler battle, like two fellows slugging it out, draws a rowdy crowd!

I key off of this when using Knight & Hale's Fighting Purr system. After working the push-peg calls for a minute, I gobble on a tube, jake yelp on a diaphragm and cutt sharply on a slate.

So doing, I've pulled in a couple of hung-up gobblers looking to get in on the action. And one day, I simulated a big turkey fight, complete with boisterous onlookers, and called in a silent longbeard that I didn't know was strutting in a hollow 100 yards away. Add realism to your aggravated purrs by gobbling, jake yelping and cutting in tandem. It makes fight calls twice as effective.

Don't Forget To Purr

Loud, aggressive calling is all the rage today, and it is effective. But often overlooked are subtle calls like the soft purr, which is deadly for closing the sale with gobblers.

The purr has a subtle, fluttering quality that signals contentment in wild turkeys. In the spring, a hen often purrs to close a sale of her own: She croons to a tom that she is over here and ready to be bred.

Soft purring on a diaphragm is effective, for it allows you to call while holding your shotgun in ready shooting position. But if you have trouble purring on a mouth yelper, as many hunters do, use a slate call.

When a gobbler closes to within 60 yards of your setup, purr ever so softly. This keeps the turkey on the move and guessing as to the precise location of the contented hen, enhancing your chances of reeling him in.

Friction In The Wind

Out in the wide-open West, where the wind often blows the camo cap off your head all day long, I've *watched* Merriam's and Rio Grande toms gobble, but couldn't hear them. It is an odd but revealing thing to see.

Yelping and cutting on boxes and slates, I've watched gobblers outstretch their necks and wobble to honor my calling. Switching to diaphragms, I've seen the same turkeys just stand there. They couldn't hear the mouth calls!

Regardless of where you turkey hunt, think friction on windy days. The loud, sharp, high-pitched notes of boxes and glass slates pierce the breeze better than diaphragms. For maximum efficiency, maneuver upwind of where you think a gobbler might be strutting and let your calls float downwind to him.

Blend Air and Friction

With turkey populations at record highs in many areas, more hens than ever are available to gobblers. While a tom once had to round up hens one by one, he now often runs across two, three or even a small flock of females in springtime.

Keying off of this to diversify your calling, try yelping on a diaphragm while clucking on a box, or cutting on a slate while purring on a tube. Toss in hollow yelps from a wingbone. The calling schemes are endless. By blending air and friction calls to imitate several hens traveling together, you can often lure a gobbler intent on gathering an instant harem.

"Break" Your Diaphragm

Realizing hens to be the ultimate calling competition, most hunters hate to hear them clucking and yelping on a spring morning. Ah, but I love listening to hens, for studying their calls is most revealing.

The more hens I listen to, the more idiosyncrasies I find in their calls. While some hens are classic high-pitched or raspy yelpers, others sound terrible. Some hens have distinctive little whines, squeals or squeaks (sounding sort of like chopped-off kee kees) in their yelping.

Forever looking for an edge, I key into this and "break" my diaphragm yelping. Amid a series of yelps, I tongue-pressure a diaphragm, pinning it tightly to the roof of my mouth for a split-second before releasing it to resume standard yelping. This injects a little squeal or whine into my calls.

When trying this, make any break short (a fraction of a second) and sweet. A subtle squeal, whine or squeak is most authentic and often the magical note that excites a gobbler and brings him your way.

Calling Busted Gobblers

Easing through the black predawn woods, you accidentally bust a turkey off its roost. The bird flaps away, big wings beating the tree limbs. You figure surely it was a gobbler.

Is your hunt ruined? Seems that way on the surface. But realize that turkeys bumped from their roosts don't like to fly very far in the dark (they have poor night vision). Many hunters think spooked turkeys fly out of the county, when in reality most sail a couple of hundred yards and alight in another tree.

If you bust a roosted bird that you believe to be a gobbler, move quietly 75 to 100 yards in the direction he flew and set up. The gobbler may sit in his second tree until well after sunup, and he probably won't gobble.

Many live hens have distinctive little whines, squeals and squeaks in their voices. Whining on a box call before beginning a yelping sequence can elicit booming gobbles from some toms.

But listen for the thumping of the turkey's wings as he pitches down, then try to jump-start him with moderately aggressive calling.

Wild turkeys have short memories. In time, a hot gobbler will forget about the roost disruption and get back into the breeding game. If you stick with him, you may be the most convenient hen in the area. He may eventually crank up his gobbling and strut in, turning a potentially busted hunt into a classic adventure.

Whine On A Box

One little trick that can elicit booming gobbles from some toms is to whine on a box call before yelping. To do this, pull the call's handle sideways into yelping position. Then press the handle firmly down on the box's sounding lip and make a short, tight stroke before moving into a yelping cadence. You'll get a squeaky, high-pitched whine that drives some gobblers crazy.

Fade Your Yelps

Each time you're in the spring woods, either scouting or hunting, listen intently to any live hens you encounter. You will note that many hens fade their yelping. Some begin to yelp softly, then crank up the volume. Other hens yelp loudly at first, then tail off with soft calling.

"Fading" on any type of call injects realism into your yelping. I like to yelp fairly loud and then fade out, making my final notes barely audible. The hard initial calling allows a gobbler to locate me. The fading yelps then have a melodious, ventriloquial effect that keeps a tom on the move and guessing precisely where I am.

In my experience, the best way to get your hands on a western gobbler is to hammer him with calling. If you tone down when working a Merriam's tom, he may lose interest and wander off in search of a more willing hen.

Hammer Western Toms

Many times it is best to hit an Eastern gobbler with loud, aggressive calling, then gradually scale back to more subtle yelping, clucking and purring to close the sale. Not so with Western turkeys in my experience.

If you tone down your calling to a Rio Grande or Merriam's gobbler, he will often lose interest and drift away. I am not positive why this occurs—I believe it is because Western hens are, by nature, highly vocal. Regardless, hammer Rios and Merriam's with aggressive calling, within reason of course, to keep then involved in your mock breeding game.

Bag Your Box Call

Perfection Calls' Jim Clay is one of the most gifted diaphragm callers in the country, yet he often uses a box to inject diversity into his calling routine. Here's a little trick he showed me for box calling on rainy mornings.

Clay carries his box in a plastic bread bag sprayed with camo paint. He never removes the call from the bag (remember, if a wooden box gets wet, it is useless), but simply reaches inside and works the call's handle to cluck, yelp or cutt. His calls might be a little muffled, but that is all right. Rainy, humid mornings deaden any type of turkey calling. So bag your box and don't be afraid to use it on wet days.

A Late-Spring Calling Setup

When you hunt the tag end of a spring season and encounter little or no gobbling activity, set up near potential hen nesting areas— power or gas line cuts, field edges, clearcuts and similar spots with dense understory. Sit against a tree, perhaps fashion a little brush blind around you and cold call for a couple of hours if you have the time and patience.

The second gobbling peak may be winding down, and toms will be skittish from weeks of hunting pressure. But you can bet a gobbler or two will be on the prowl for leftover hens to breed. A tom naturally checks for hens near prominent nesting areas. If you set up and call sweetly nearby, he just might find you.

Stick With Drumming Gobblers

In springtime, hen calls are the ultimate gobbling stimuli. A gobbler may bellow at your yelps and clucks, but not be willing to make the final commitment—unless he is drumming.

Anytime you encounter a gobbling turkey, listen intently. If the tom is hanging up and giving you trouble, gobbling hard but not drumming, you may want to leave him and go look for a hotter bird.

If, however, the turkey drums as intensely as he gobbles, read this to mean he is seriously into the mating game. Sit tight and continue to work a gobbling-and-drumming turkey. There is a better than 50-50 chance he will eventually break your way.

If you cannot cut off a moving gobbler, stay hot on his heels. Crow call as you go to keep tabs on the wandering turkey. When he finally stops in a strut zone, set up and work him with hen calls.

Dog A Gobbler

One spring my brother-in-law Brian McCoy and I ran across a tough turkey in southwest Virginia. The old devil treated us to a thrilling chorus of raucous gobbling on the roost. He pitched out and failed to commit an inch to my pleading yelps, clucks and purrs, even though I knew he had no hens.

"That turkey's been fooled with," I whispered to Brian. Remember that one. It is your best excuse when a solo gobbler whips your butt.

Finally the turkey said to heck with you guys and drifted up a mountainside. We tried to circle around in front of him, but he was moving too fast, gobbling like crazy and going straight away.

"Let's dog that turkey," I told Brian. He was game, so away we went, following in the gobbler's tracks and calling spiritedly to keep tabs on him.

That old mountain warrior was a curious bird. He neglected all hen calls, but shook the foliage with thunderous gobbles every third time I crow called. Caw one, silence. Caw again, nothing. Caw a third time, *gaaaarrrraoobbbble!*

We dogged that turkey for over an hour. Every time he roared at my third crow call, we moved fast, sweating up steep mountains and gliding down ridges, carefully keeping our distance so the turkey would not twist his periscope back and spot us following in the rolling terrain. The last time the gobbler hammered my third caws, he was cresting a high, sunlit knoll.

"That's a perfect strutting place," I said to Brian, and he agreed. I switched to a mouth diaphragm and cutt sharply. *Gaaaar-rrraoobbbble!* I cutt again just to make sure, and the gobbler roared back from the same spot.

We had stopped the turkey! Actually, he had stopped on his own and was now trying mightily to call us up the knoll to him. We obliged, circling around the mountain and topping out above the knoll, where Brian finally killed the bird.

If you cannot get in front of a fast-moving gobbler (a common occurrence) try dogging him. It is a lot like pressuring a bugling bull elk. Use a locator call to keep tabs on the bird—he must gobble frequently and reveal his travel corridor for this tactic to work. If and when he finally stops in a strategic place to strut, set up and switch to hen calling to reel him in.

Realistic Cackling

Pump realism and excitement into your fly-down calls each morning by backing up your cackles with clucks. Live hens always do this, cackling spiritedly as they pitch from trees, then clucking sharply to softly as they gather themselves after the short flight. Back-up clucks are not vital for success, but they add authenticity to your calling and might be the little notes that bring a gobbler running.

Kee-Kee In The Spring

The kee-kee and kee-kee run are used primarily by lost young turkeys in fall and winter. But young hens and jakes sometimes kee-kee in the spring as well, so you should toss a few lost calls into your routine.

Several times in this chapter, we have talked about how little hen whines and squeals strike a magical chord with some toms. Kee-kees—high-pitched, melodious "pee, pee, pee" whistles—fit right in with this theory.

Adding a short yelp to the end of your kee-kees mimics a young gobble looking for company. A dominant tom might not want a crazy jake floating around his breeding zone, so he might roar his disapproval at your kee-kee-run and come in to check it out.

The easiest way to kee-kee is on a single-frame diaphragm with one or two reeds. I sometimes kee-kee on a slate for lost notes that sound a little unique. Hold a wooden peg tightly and work near an outer edge of a slate cup to produce three high- pitched kee-kees. Pull the striker down toward the middle of the call to back up your whistles with a jake yawk.

Gobble First

Most hunters try challenging a dominant, henned-up tom with gobbling only as a last resort. But sometimes it pays to hit a difficult bird with a good dose of gobbler medicine first thing in the morning.

Here's the situation. You hunt the same gobbler three mornings in a row. He roars at your yelping, but flies down and hang ups or marches away with his hens. You've tried maneuvering around on him to no avail. You need a desperate measure.

While the kee-kee and kee-kee run are primarily fall calls, whistling on a diaphragm in the spring strikes a chord with some gobblers.

As dawn breaks on the fourth day of battle, set up tight and wait for the turkeys to fly down. Listen for the thumping of heavy wings or a foliage-muffled gobble to tell you a tom is on the ground. Then hit the flock with a thunderous gobble from a tube call or rubber shaker.

The gobbler will definitely do a double take and think, "Who's that invading my turf?" He will likely become agitated and roar a gobble to suppress you with his dominance. Try gobbling once more to tell him you're here to say. The turkey might eventually run over to kick your butt, allowing you to turn the tables on him.

One thing to remember: Don't gobble while the tom and his hens are still in their trees. If you do, the gobbler will likely sit up there scanning the woods for the vagabond tom. Seeing no feathers of his potential foe, he and his hens may pitch out and move away even faster than on previous mornings.

It pays to sit tight and wait out a sporadically gobbling turkey for a hour or more. By wearing on an old tom's patience, you can often make him break strut and commit to your calls.

Chapter 9

Sit Tight Or Move?

Here are two of the most common and frustrating scenarios in spring turkey hunting.

You steal like a thief through the misty predawn to within 100 yards of gobbler's roost tree. The turkey sweeps from his limb and honors your calling with a hard-hearted gobble or two, but fails to move an inch in your direction.

Cutting and running through the sun-glistening woods at mid-morning, you strike a tom, set up and yelp. The gobbler roars his approval, nearly blowing the camo cap off your head. The turkey runs your way, and you're all excited and ready to close the sale. Then your heart sinks as he slams on the brakes and plants himself to the terra firma 75 yards away, gobbling all the while.

In either situation, the gobbler is hung up and you are faced with a big-time dilemma. Do you sit tight and wait out the turkey, or do you make a fancy move on him?

Reading Gobbler Hang-Ups

For starters, remain seated in your calling position and listen intently. Try to read a turkey's gobbling to determine just what type of hard-headed bird you're up against.

A turkey that gobbles passionately at your calls but hangs up just out of shotgun range is likely a hot two-year-old. Amid breaks in his gobbling, listen for drumming. You should be able to hear the *pfftt, duuummm* for 60 to 100 yards, depending on terrain, ground foliage and wind conditions. In my experience, a two-year-old tom that hangs up in dead strut drums as intensely as he gobbles.

Most three-, four-, and five-year-old turkeys don't do a ton of gobbling on the ground. And an old tom typically drums in short spits— *pffts*—as he pops into half strut, then folds his tail feathers quickly. This allows him to scan 360 degrees of greening woods for willing hens and skulking predators, including hunters.

As you zero in a turkey's gobbling and drumming, listen intently for the clucking, purring and yelping of hens. In addition to hunting pressure, predators and an unknown hazard in the area (fence, creek, ditch, strip of brush, etc.) hens are often the culprit that hangs up gobblers.

Having reasonably determined whether you're working a lusty two-year-old turkey or a crafty old gobbler with or without hens, you're primed to key a variety of sit-tight or maneuvering strategies to the task at hand.

A hot two-year-old tom struts and drums as intensely as he gobbles. If a turkey suddenly quits gobbling, listen closely for his drumming before moving. The bird might be slipping in to your calls. (Photo courtesy Perfection Turkey Calls)

When To Play The Waiting Game

Anytime you run across a sporadically gobbling old turkey, it pays to wait him out for at least 30 minutes and possibly as long as two hours if you have the time and patience. A wise bird hasn't kept his beard and spurs intact for three years or longer by gobbling at and running to every call hunters make.

Upon honoring your yelping with a rousing gobble, a dominant turkey often half-struts in a spot with good visibility and looks hard for the calling hen. He may or may not have ladies, and there might not be an obstacle out there to hang him up. The gobbler's just taking his time, playing the courtship game and waiting for you to come to him.

By remaining planted firmly against a tree, you wear on an old turkey's patience. He is wise and skittish, but ready, willing and certainly able to breed every hot little hen in his strut zone. By varying your calling from passive to aggressive and scratching in the leaves to mimic a pacing hen for an hour or more, you can often make a gobbler think you're the only gal in town. He may then break his half strut and commit your way.

If you determine that a hung-up gobbler has hens, this is definitely the time to sit tight for an extended period of time. Try to rile a boss hen with spirited yelping, clucking and cutting. If she responds, mimic her calls with loud and aggressive series of your own. The agitated hens may eventually stroll over to check you out, bringing an old gobbler with them.

If calling fails to produce, shut up for 30 minutes or so. Then test the gobbler with one sharp yelp or cutt. If he doesn't respond, sit awhile longer, hoping the hens will finally drift off to lay or sit atop eggs. If this occurs, the gobbler will remember where you are, and he might slip in silently.

Anytime a hung-up turkey suddenly quits gobbling, don't move for at least 10 minutes. Sitting still for 15 or 20 minutes, listening for low-frequency drumming and the sounds of turkey feet shuffling leaves, is better insurance yet. The gobbler might finally be coming, taking his time and strutting in. Most hunters move much too quickly when gobblers fall silent—and so doing, bust turkeys that are working to their calls!

When you're dueling a hard-gobbling turkey, especially on public land, another hunter might blunder in and bump the bird. Or a pack of howling wild dogs might shut him up. Or a bobcat that you cannot see or hear might slink in and spook the gobbler. Frustrating scenarios to be sure. But if you know or sense that a predator has spooked a turkey you are working on, remain set up silently for an hour or so.

The hunter, dogs or cat will eventually leave, and once this occurs, you can often revive a seemingly ill-fated hunt. Once danger passes, a turkey ripe with the rut often regains his confidence and goes back to gobbling, either on his own or in response to your calling. A spooked bird may even feel a security need to consort with one of his own, making him come quickly to investigate your calls.

When To Move

One spring in Virginia, I sneaked within 100 yards of a strutting turkey, set up with my back to an oak tree and yelped softly on a slate call. The two-year-old triple gobbled, honoring me as a hen with his ultimate mating call. The turkey then ran my way, stopped 70 yards out, roared in my face and marched 100 yards back up the hardwood ridge. He repeated his parade three times, always returning to the same spot to gobble in my direction.

Like many gobblers I have encountered in 30 years of serious turkey hunting, an unknown hazard, in this case a three-foot-wide ditch, had served as a stone wall to hang up the hot bird.

Anytime a gobbler begins drifting steadily away from your setup, move quickly to cut him off. Once a tom makes up his mind to leave an area, it is almost impossible to turn him back with calling.

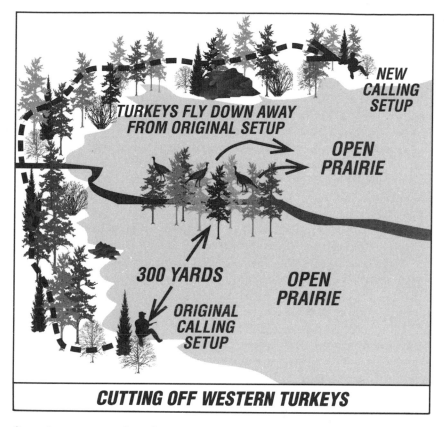

CUTTING OFF WESTERN TURKEYS

Sometimes you are forced to set up several hundred yards away from Merriam's or Rio Grandes roosted in sparse trees in an open prairie, park or meadow. If the turkeys fly down at dawn and move away from your yelping, quickly make a wide circle, using available cover to hide your moves, and relocate to a calling position in front of the traveling turkeys. Attempting to call back western gobblers that beeline to feeding, strutting or watering grounds first thing in the morning is a doomed strategy.

When the turkey retreated up the ridge for the fourth time, I slipped back 50 yards, circled 300 yards around and set up 180 degrees from my original calling position. I yelped once and the longbeard ran in gobbling all the way.

Most gobblers who encounter a hazard that they are not willing to come across or through exhibit similar behavior. Strutting back and forth, they stop on the doorstep of a creek, ditch or fence to gobble in hopes the hen will come to them. When you run across this type of stuck-up bird, you should move.

Before you do, however, devise a strategic game plan. As you sit and call to the turkey, scan the terrain, mentally draw a line to a fresh calling location and determine precisely where you want to go. Then get up and move quickly on the off chance that the gobbler will drop strut and hop a ditch or fly a creek or fence. This is the exception rather the rule, but it does happen, especially when working hot two-year-old toms sans hens. If you tarry, you just might spook a turkey taking an inconvenient route into your calls.

Anytime a gobbler you're working drifts steadily away from your yelping, his gobbles growing fainter and fainter by the minute, hotfoot it out of there. Once an Eastern gobbler makes up his mind to go somewhere, it's tough to change his line of travel with calling. And in my experience, it is virtually impossible to call back Rio Grande or Merriam's turkeys, which often beeline for miles to preferred feeding, watering, strutting and roosting areas each day.

Move quickly, circling far and wide to cut off a walking gobbler. Try to reposition somewhere along his travel corridor or, better yet, set up in a strutting, feeding or roosting area where the turkey ultimately wants to end up for the day.

Whenever you're set up slightly below a gobbler who hangs on a ridge, knoll or bluff, it is time to move. As mentioned in the previous chapter, it's always best to yelp to a turkey from the same level or slightly above him.

Maneuvering Strategies

As a rule, the better you know the lay of the land you're hunting, the quicker you should move on a turkey. By slipping over familiar terrain and relocating to a relatively open spot where you know a gobbler will feel safe and comfortable traveling and strutting, you double your odds of success.

Conversely, if you're working virgin ground, be a little more patient. Move too quickly and you might blunder into an unknown logging road, field edge or similar opening where a hung-up gobbler on the lookout for hens and danger will see you. You might even relocate to an obstacle-laced area that is even worse than your original setup, greatly decreasing your odds of luring a bird.

Before moving on a turkey, always pinpoint his location. A gobbler often sounds farther away than he really is because of lush ground foliage or wrinkles in the terrain. Also, a turkey that spins around and gobbles directly away from you may sound 100 yards away when he's really only 75 steps distant. Wait for a turkey to gobble in your direction or zero in on his drumming before relocating.

If you can eyeball a turkey strutting 100 yards or so away in a field, river bottom or mature stand of hardwoods, you can bet he will nail you if you make a foolish, ill-timed maneuver. When a gobbler is in sight, it's best not to move at all, but sometimes you must.

When the turkey drifts behind a patch of brush or a fallen tree, crawl straight back, using foliage and any rise or dip in the terrain to cover your movements. A prime time to maneuver is when a gobbler turns his fanned tail to you and swings to the far end of his strut zone, where he is momentarily out of sight.

Most of the time, you'll move on gobblers that you cannot see because of dense foliage or breaks in the terrain. Still, slip cautiously 50 to 100 yards back, using available cover to your advantage.

Then make a big, wide circle, forever looking for an open chute where a gobbler may feel comfortable strutting into your calls. I sometimes yelp or cutt aggressively as I move. I want the gobbler to answer so I can monitor his location. But even if he doesn't respond, he may think the hen is coming to him in a roundabout way, especially if he hears the shuffling of leaves as I sneak along.

When maneuvering on a sharp-eyed gobbler, make wide circles, stay low and use any available cover to disguise your movements.

There is a risk to yelping on the move, however. A gobbler at some point might fold strut and break toward your calls. You may spook him or lure him to an inhospitable place where it is impossible to close the sale. It's really best to owl hoot or crow call as you move to keep tabs on a turkey.

Pinpointing a gobbler's location at all times is paramount, since you should slip in as tightly as possible in an attempt to fire him up

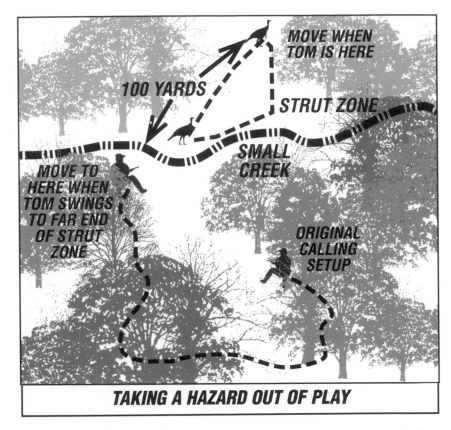

TAKING A HAZARD OUT OF PLAY

A tom that encounters a creek, fence or ditch will often hang up on the door step of the hazard, gobble like crazy at your calls, retreat 100 yards or so, then return to the same spot to gobble again. He's trying to call the hen across the obstacle to him. In this case, wait until the turkey walks off a second or third time, move quickly forward, set up near or beyond the hazard and intercept the gobbler as he struts back your way.

with fresh calling from a new spot. You may have to set up 150 yards away from a bird in the leafless, early-spring woods, but closing to 100 paces is always better. Late in the season, you can often slip within 80 yards or so of a gobbler when the ground foliage is in full bloom.

Crouch and sneak on your final approach, belly-crawl the last 20 yards and set up quickly. Think back to your original setup—was it a yelp, cluck or cutt that really turned the gobbler on? From your new location, hit the turkey with the call you know he prefers. He'll likely gobble and he just might come running.

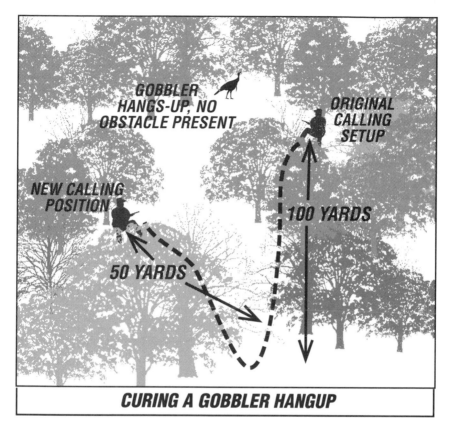

GOBBLER HANGS-UP, NO OBSTACLE PRESENT

ORIGINAL CALLING SETUP

NEW CALLING POSITION

100 YARDS

50 YARDS

CURING A GOBBLER HANGUP

When a gobbler hangs up, try moving 100 yards straight back, yelping and cutting aggressively and shuffling leaves as you go. Then sneak 50 to 75 yards back toward the turkey, set up off to one side of your original position and get ready—but refrain from calling again. Nervous that the finicky hen is leaving the area, the gobbler may break to follow her, allowing you to cut him off.

Most of the time, it is best to maneuver to one side of a gobbler and circle around to get in front of him. But here are two fancy vertical moves that can pay off.

If you think a gobbler has hit a hazard, wait for him to strut directly away from you. Then maneuver quickly 20 or 30 yards forward and set up within shotgun range of the obstacle or, better yet, just beyond it. By taking a creek, fence, ditch or other hazard out of play, you can often ambush a turkey as he swings back in your direction.

Moving back on a hung-up gobbler, yelping and scratching leaves as you go, is a time-tested and effective trick. The turkey thinks the hen is leaving, so he often breaks to follow her. But maneuvering

I relocated five times before finally calling in this big Rio Grande. Many gobblers are un-callable unless you move to an area where they feel comfortable strutting.

backwards puts more ground between you and a gobbler. There is a good chance he'll strut in for a closer look, then hang up from your calling a second time.

To alleviate this problem, I add a twist to the back-up routine. After moving 100 yards or so away from a gobbler, yelping as I go, I turn, slip 50 to 75 yards back toward the turkey, set up and never call again. Thinking the hen is leaving, a gobbler may stroll closer to take a peek, and I can often cut him off. When trying this technique, remember never to call from your new setup. If you do, the gobbler will likely hang up again.

A Final Moving Thought

Whether to sit tight or move on a hung-up gobbler is a gut decision that you will be forced to make hundreds of times during your turkey hunting career. Each situation and each individual turkey is different.

I am an aggressive turkey hunter and tend to move on ornery gobblers that give me half a chance. This has proved highly successful over the years, but I've also busted my share of gobblers.

For this reason, I often wish I would slow down in the spring woods and do as an Alabama turkey guide once told me. Both you and I would do well to heed his advice.

"Some situations are cut and dried, you just gotta move if you expect to kill a turkey," old Joe said. "But if you're the least bit indecisive about whether or not to move, that's when you'll spook a turkey and ruin the game. If you have a little patience, you can always come back and hunt him tomorrow morning."

I encountered this big tom traveling with three hens. He gobbled only once, but strutted and drummed intensely into my passive calling.

Chapter 10

Silent Toms

Spring gobbler hunting is a peak and valley affair. Depending on which region of the country you hunt, gobbling intensifies in March or April as dominant toms, spurred on by lengthening daylight hours and warming weather, call lustily to gather harems of hens.

The gobbling apex may last several days or a week and is nirvana for the turkey caller. During this phase, you should hit the woods every morning if possible. Traveling widely and booming gobbles on their own to attract as many hens as possible, longbeards may break their necks racing in to your calls.

The two-week gobbling lull occurs when receptive hens travel with dominant longbeards. This is a tough time to call in a turkey. (Photo courtesy Perfection Turkey Calls)

Ah, but the dreaded gobbling lull lies right around the corner. As alpha gobblers encircle their gaudy selves with hens and suppress many (but not all) two-year-old males, gobbling frequency decreases dramatically. The old boys with mates at their beck and call have little reason to talk. And having had their tail feathers kicked by superior birds, many inferior toms are scared to death to gobble. For the caller, the silent woods are purgatory.

Should you hang up your calls and lie in bed each morning, catching up on much needed rest and waiting for the second gobbling peak to occur as impregnated hens desert the toms to nest? No way. Here are some strategies that will help you score when gobblers fall silent.

The Active Approach

Often referred to as "cutting and running," the active technique involves covering lots of country and calling aggressively to force the action. When turkeys are loathe to gobble, you must shock them into talking.

Cutting and running can be effective whether you hunt several small farms or a huge chunk of public ground. In the former scenario, drive to a piece of private property at daybreak and locator call and hen yelp from a couple of strategic listening posts. If you fail to entice a turkey into gobbling, a distinct possibility, motor off to another farm and repeat the calling process. Cutt and run until you exhaust all of your hunting spots.

If you hunt big country, say a 1,000-acre or larger tract of private or public land, drive around the perimeter of the area if possible. Stop frequently and locator call and cutt on a box or slate in hopes of pulling a single gobble from a bird.

If no roads rim the property, which in most cases is good news since this minimizes your hunting competition, hike logging two-tracks, power-line cuts, horse or foot trails, field edges and similar routes that allow you to cover miles of country as quickly and as efficiently as possible first thing each morning. Pause every couple of hundred yards and call sharply in hopes of striking a gobbler.

Here's an active hunt in motion. From a good vantage at first light, owl hoot aggressively. Go crazy on a crow call to mimic a pair of black bandits aggravating an owl or a turkey, or fighting each other. Cut loose a couple of coyote yips and howls. You need more shocking power than normal to startle tight-lipped turkeys into talking.

Raising nary a peep, turn to yelping and cutting in loud and lively series on a diaphragm, box, slate or tube call. On the run, I like

Covering lots of ground while locator calling and cutting aggressively is a good way to find a hot tom and pull a gobble or two out of him.

to yelp and cutt on a box. And I really hammer a hickory striker against a synthetic-glass or aluminum-plated "slate."

In my experience, a friction call's sharp, piercing notes carry farther than even the loudest diaphragm, thus creating greater potential for shocking gobbles from silent turkeys roosted or strutting several hundred yards away. Many hunters married to mouth calls fail to realize this. If this is you, continue to use your favorite diaphragms, but toss in some spirited friction calling to double your responses from close-mouthed toms.

Probe the woods with the finest friction calling on earth, and things may remain as quiet as a tomb during the gobbling lull. Frustrating, but no big deal if you persevere. Drive or walk several hundred yards and repeat your spirited locator calling and cutting sequences. Prospect as far and wide as possible within the legal boundaries of your hunting turf.

As you move, keep one very important factor in mind. To make a henned-up tom or a suppressed two-year-old gobble, you must often locator call or cutt within 125 yards of him. It's not called the gobbling lull for nothing. Call to a silent tom standing hidden in the foliage a couple of hundred yards away, and he may stare in your direction but fail to open his beak.

By traveling widely and pausing frequently to call, you increase your odds of striking a turkey. If you run across a silent and unseen gobbler roosted or strutting 80 to 100 yards away, your spirited calling may act as a stimulus that causes him to shock gobble, even though he doesn't really want to.

During the lull, I think that turkeys who gobble on reflex probably pull their necks frantically back into their bodies and say to themselves, "Oh no, why did I do that!" This while you're diving for the nearest setup tree, all excited and whispering to yourself, "Yeesss!"

When a henned-up old tom roars at your calls, you've still got your camouflaged hands full. He may simply refuse to work. But when a two-year-old gobbler hot to breed a hen responds, smile all over yourself. The turkey might run to your calls at breakneck speed. For this reason, anytime you strike a gobbler close, set up quickly, fine-tune your shooting position and be ready.

The Passive Strategy

Think back to all the preseason scouting you did. The areas you are now fixing to hunt via a passive strategy held lots of tracks, droppings, strut marks and other turkey sign. And you probably heard gobbling in the vicinity a week or so earlier as dominant toms gathered their hens. All of this should give you confidence to know that the longbeards are still out there, even though they are as quiet as mice at a cat show.

At dawn, try the aggressive locator calling and cutting techniques detailed in the previous section. If these calls fail to produce, that is all right. Slip into areas that you know hold turkeys, and set up in oak flats, canyon bottoms, creek drainages, field edges or similar spots where gobblers prefer to travel and strut. Then run through a couple of cold-calling routines.

Start out with moderately aggressive clucking, yelping and cutting to simulate a hen hitting the ground and pacing around, looking to hook up with a gobbler. Then lay down your call and sit quietly for 30 minutes or so.

While a nearby tom might not gobble at your calls, he may strut in your direction. Your initial calling sequence allows him to home in on your general location. The lull in your yelping then gives him a good dose of his own medicine. If he closes to within 100 yards or so and fails to see a hen, he might get impatient and boom a gobble, hoping to draw her out of the cover.

Anytime you force a silent turkey to gobble once, refrain from calling for a while. His interest piqued, the turkey might drift into

Cold calling for an hour or longer in a well-scouted woodland that you know holds turkeys is an excellent way to score during the gobbling lull.

shotgun range on his own. If the bird fails to show in 10 minutes or so, toss him a few soft clucks and purrs in hopes of reeling him in.

If your initial calling sequence fails to roust a gobble, try clucking, yelping and purring every 20 minutes or so. Remain seated and call softly for an hour or two if you have the time and the patience. Many hunters, myself included, often have the time but lack the self-discipline to cold call in silent woods. This is a huge mistake, for the simplest of all turkey hunting tactics makes all the sense in the world. Set up in an area littered with turkey sign and sound like a hen, and odds are a gobbler will stroll in sooner or later to check you out.

While I have lured a few dominant gobblers with passive calling over the years, I find the technique most effective, dynamite really, for two-year-old toms. Remember, the longbeards are out there, keeping their distance from dominant birds but traveling widely and on the lookout for a golden opportunity to breed a hen.

Reluctant to reveal their intentions to a boss bird, a two-year-old may gobble only once or twice or not at all, but they will come. So level your shotgun over your knee and be still as you soft-call. Cut only your eyes as you scan the foliage for the tip of a fanned tail or a flaming red head and neck. Drop your guard, and a silent tom will bust you every time and add further to the frustrations of the gobbling lull.

Most places I hunt today, I find subordinate longbeards traveling with dominant strutters and breeders. Every time you set up to call a gobbling turkey, remember that you may be working a fringe tom as well. (Photo courtesy Mossy Oak)

Chapter 11

Fooling Fringe Gobblers

In the previous chapter, I mentioned that as dominant gobblers gather their hens in March and April, they challenge and suppress many, but not all, inferior toms. "But not all" are the key words to be carried over into this discussion. You see, the fact that boss gobblers are tolerating and traveling with subordinate toms as never before is a growing phenomenon in spring turkey country.

As recently as 10 years ago, long-spurred gobblers assembling their harems had little difficulty intimidating and running off the few jakes and inferior two-year-old toms that were brazen or foolish enough to venture into their breeding ranges. But with record numbers of gobblers per square mile in many states today, boss birds would have to spend the entire mating season challenging subordinates.

The bosses have something much more important and intriguing on their minds, namely procreating with as many hot little hens as possible. The old birds try madly to intimidate the omega toms with aggressive gobbling and aggravated purring, and engage in some vicious sparring matches with potential rivals. But in the end, many dominant gobblers are forced to allow "fringe" toms to travel in proximity to them.

Over the past decade, I have been fortunate enough to hunt some of the best-managed private lands across Eastern, Osceola, Rio Grande and Merriam's range. I've also called on some of the finest public turkey ground in America. In many regions, I have found that it is difficult if not impossible to find a mature gobbler traveling alone during any phase of the breeding season. I expect that this dilemma will only grow as wild turkeys continue to expand their population and range across North America.

This means that in many instances, you must focus your strategy on hunting and calling dominant gobblers traveling not only with hens, but also with perimeter toms. Here's how to do it.

Fringe Turkey Setups

The typical scenario is for one or two subordinate gobblers to work the perimeter of a boss turkey's harem, waiting for an opportunity to slip in and breed a hen. Sometimes I think a dominant gobbler allows a longbeard—likely a sibling or a close buddy from the fall flock—to travel by his side. The old turkey gobbles, struts and breeds the hens, while his partner acts as both sentry and bodyguard, looking for potential danger and even challenging other toms traveling the fringe.

On the surface, fringe gobblers seem ripe for the picking. With several hot-to-trot longbeards working an area, there is an excellent chance one will respond to your sweet hens calls, right? Well, this is sometimes the case. But fringe gobblers can also cause a lot of trouble.

Each time you set up, consider that the wonderful gobbling you hear is likely that of a dominant bird. But remember, odds are good that one or more inferior toms, which normally don't gobble much if at all, will hear your calling as well. Keep your guard up and be ready for a fringe gobbler to sneak in to your calls. Focus solely on a

With record numbers of wild turkeys out there today, many dominant gobblers are forced to allow fringe birds to travel with them. If you spot a pair of gobblers strutting wing to wing, it is a good bet they are brothers. (Photo courtesy Perfection Turkey Calls)

hard-gobbling turkey, and you'll often fail to see a perimeter tom slipping in, typically off to one side of you. You may shift your body, move your hands to work a box or slate call or wave your shotgun barrel around, spooking the bird.

Another mistake you might make is to relocate too quickly on a gobbling bird that hangs up. You may unsuspectingly blunder into a fringe tom, which will then putt, run or fly, busting all the turkeys in the vicinity.

To counteract such dilemmas, listen intently every time you set up to call. You must determine if, how many, and precisely where inferior gobblers are working the perimeter of a spring flock.

Pinpoint the gobbling tom, then listen for gobbler talk on the fringes. While inferior longbeards rarely gobble, they often drum, cluck deeply or yelp slowly and coarsely. Jakes are prone to "short gobble," but don't be fooled. Some young gobblers roar as lustily as dominant birds.

When working fringe gobblers, I normally sit awhile in one spot and hen cluck, yelp and cutt aggressively. Sometimes I use Knight & Hale's Fighting Purr while gobbling on a

Aggressive fight calling can often rile up dominant and fringe gobblers and cause them to break your way.

tube call. I try to stir up all the turkeys in an area. In time, a fired-up inferior gobbler might sneak in for a look. If I'm really lucky, the dominant bird might stroll over with several subordinate birds in tow.

When I feel it is time to relocate, I normally move 50 to 100 yards back and off to one side where I hear the coarse clucking and yelping of one or more fringe birds. Here's my theory: If I can lure an inferior tom 100 yards or so away from a dominant bird, into a zone where he feels comfortable and confident strutting for a hen and perhaps even booming a gobble or two, I can kill him a good percentage of the time.

In Virginia several springs ago, I yelped in a gobbler for my good friend and outdoor editor Tom Fulgham, who deftly maneuvered his Remington 870 around a sapling and rolled the turkey neatly with a load of Number 5s. As we raced out to admire Tom's prize, another gobbler roared less than 70 yards away. We sped back to our calling site, dead turkey in tow, and dove for cover. I called the gobbling jake, who sounded like the bull of the woods, to within 20 yards, but let him walk. We could have killed a pair of gobblers from the same tree in less than five minutes.

With multiple longbeards using the same home ranges today, it is quite possible to double from one location if you hunt wisely. If your partner shoots a gobbler, retrieve his bird quickly and set up

ISOLATING FRINGE GOBBLERS

Always listen for a fringe gobbler clucking, drumming and perhaps gobbling a time or two off to one side of a dominant tom with hens. If the boss bird won't work to your calls, relocate near the subdominant gobbler and give him some soft yelping, clucking and purring. It's often possible to lure a fringe longbeard to an out-of-the-way spot where he thinks he can breed a hen.

With many gobblers inhabiting the same home ranges today, it is often possible to double from the same setup. After your partner shoots his turkey, remain seated and try to start a fringe gobbler with aggressive hen calling or gobbler yelping.

again. Turkeys cannot rationalize that what they just heard was the booming of a hunter's shotgun. In fact, they just might shock gobble at it.

Wait for the woods to settle down and try to start a fringe gobbler with aggressive yelping or gobbler calling. Luring a second gobbler to the same tree where you killed the first one is a bit unusual, but maneuvering to a nearby calling setup and completing your double is a distinct possibility.

The Leave-Him-Alone Tactic

Several springs ago, I visited Bent Creek Lodge in western Alabama, one of the premier turkey hunting lodges in the Southeast. Early one morning, I piled into a pickup with two friends, Mossy Oak camo designer Toxey Haas and Bent Creek guide Larry Norton. We felt all giddy as we prepared to set a combined 75-plus years of turkey hunting experience into motion. We vowed to return for breakfast with at least one sharp-spurred tom slug proudly over our collective shoulders.

We encountered a hard-gobbling turkey roosted in a creek bottom and gave him every type of hen calling known to man. He flew down with a bevy of hens and several inferior, coarse-clucking toms. The spring flock milled around awhile before marching straight away from our expert calling. Just to get under our skin, the old turkey tossed us a cursory gobble.

"Let's leave that turkey alone and come back for him later," Norton whispered, fire in his eyes. Haas and I nodded the affirmative and vowed to return with a vengeance.

"Leaving him alone" is another excellent strategy for dealing with a gobbler and his traveling companions. By midmorning, an old bird's hens often leave him for the nest. And inferior gobblers, having watched the boss strut and breed hens all morning, are at once frustrated and highly stimulated. Return to an area, cutt aggressively and odds are great that a gobbler or two will respond.

When we sneaked back into the creek bottom at 10:00 a.m., Norton cutt on a diaphragm call. A turkey roared 300 yards away.

Alabama turkey guide Larry Norton (right) and I encountered a spring flock one April morning. We left to let the turkeys do their thing, then returned at 10:00 a.m. Three fringe gobblers with ground-dragging beards raced into our calls, and I nailed one of them.

We cut the distance 100 yards and paused for Haas to yelp. The turkey gobbled on the dead run 80 yards out.

In Chinese fire drill mode, we dove for cover. Just to say I did something, I yelped softly on a diaphragm, leveled my Mossberg autoloader over my knee and focused on a pair of brilliant white heads jerking through the green foliage.

Huge wings touching, the dominant gobbler and an inferior friend body-rocked in as fast as two turkeys can come. I set my sights on the old bird, who paused at 40 yards to gobble and strut. As he did, his loyal buddy shot up his fiery red neck and scanned the ground cover for the calling hen.

I then cut my eyes to movement on the left fringe—a third gobbler with a ground-dragging rope was sneaking in! I learned the hard way a long time ago never to pass up a big turkey in hopes of killing a bigger one. Too many things can and will go wrong, and you will be left cussing and holding the proverbial bag. I eased the Mossberg slowly left and rolled the three-year-old gobbler at 20 paces, completing yet another intriguing hunt for fringe turkeys.

I hunted this bad gobbler for five days in a row. "The Wizard" had only a fair-size beard and weighed a whopping 16 3/4 pounds.

Chapter 12

Bad Turkeys

You're apt to run across at least one "bad turkey" each spring. Here's the devil I'm talking about.

The turkey may gobble once or twice on the limb every other morning. Or he might roar passionately on the roost each dawn before pitching down and going as tight-lipped as a teenage boy at his first school dance. In either scenario, just to get your goat, the tom will toss you a cursory gobble or two as he tucks his tail feathers and marches defiantly away from your sweetest yelping.

As a bad turkey vanishes into the thin, gray air each morning, his reputation grows and grows. The mystical bird soon becomes a legend with local hunters, who give him a name like Black Magic, Houdini or The Wizard. All sorts of fitting but unprintable monikers are hung on obstinate gobblers.

Once a turkey turns bad enough to warrant a name, hunting him turns from leisurely fun to war-like obsession. You can duel a bad gobbler for days or weeks in hopes of glimpsing his white head and swinging beard. Heaven forbid, you may spend an entire spring season hearing him gobble on the roost but never seeing him on the ground.

So why in the world hunt a seemingly unkillable bird? For me, it goes straight to the core of the spring obsession. Chasing an unpredictable and irregular gobbling turkey with an amazing repertoire of evasive maneuvers is the ultimate challenge. Nothing compares with finally coaxing the old boy into shotgun range.

The Nature of a Bad Bird

The term bad turkey was coined in the Southeast, where hunting notoriously tough Eastern and Osceola gobblers in the heart of their ancestral range is the rule rather than the exception. Ah, but I've run into many sporadically gobbling and aloof Rio Grande and Merriam's toms over the years. Bad turkeys are universal.

Wherever he is found, a mean turkey is three years of age or older. Instinctively skittish the moment he pecks through his egg-shell, he hones his wariness over the years as he eludes predators and survives the myriad of other perils in his outdoor world. To top things off, he turns bad to the bone for the following reasons.

First is hunting pressure. Each spring, a turkey with a catchy name and a lofty reputation is hammered with calling by a legion of hunters intent on dethroning the king of the woods and becoming local legends themselves. A bad bird whips all comers, but he is spooked almost every day. He might even have to head- duck a load of Number 4 shot on occasion. The result? A product of too many close encounters with lead poisoning, the turkey continues to gobble on the limb, but shuts up on the ground where danger lurks.

With wild turkey numbers at all-time highs in many states today, it doesn't take a nuclear scientist to figure out that record numbers of sexually mature gobblers are surrounded by record numbers of hot hens during most phases of the spring breeding season. The hen factor is another thing that turns turkeys bad.

A bad turkey is an old turkey with sharp spurs at least 1 1/4 inches long. You won't fine many hooks better than these.

A dominant gobbler roars on the roost to rally his hens and to exude his machismo over subordinate toms. When he flies down, his hens pitch down to him. A bad turkey, who has no earthly reason to gobble on the ground, just struts and drums around his ladies each morning.

Then the gobbler typically drifts away from your yelping, most often taken in that direction by an old boss hen who has heard enough of you—she hates the calling competition you throw into the mix! Following her lead, the aloof turkey often gives you a muffled gobble as if to ask, "You coming along or what? We're out of here."

So a bad turkey is an old, inherently skittish, pressure-wary, henned-up devil. And while most hunters assume he is a 20-pound bruiser of a bird with a rope-thick beard and long, sharp spurs, the opposite is often the case. A mean turkey has grandiose hooks to be sure, but he is often a 16-pound lightweight with a scraggly beard. The gobbler loses weight and rubs his beard thin while procreating with all those hens, giving him even more character.

Bad-Turkey Setups

The one chink in a tough turkey's armor is that he generally roosts and struts in a relatively small zone where he feels safe and comfortable gathering hens and eluding predators, hunters included. In Eastern and Osceola range, this zone is typically a creek bottom, swamp, hardwood hollow, oak flat or field edge. Western gobblers roost and display for hens in oak mottes, canyon bottoms and mountain meadows.

A gobbler's homebound nature plays into your camouflaged hands, for once you run across the turkey one morning, he will be in the same area the next morning and the next and the next. . . . Still, his unpredictable gobbling and rebellious behavior spell trouble. How do you pinpoint an old bird's roost tree and slip in tight without busting him each day?

Two keys to success: Arrive early, an hour before the silvery light of dawn seeps into the woods, and vary your approach angles to the turkey.

As mentioned, every serious hunter who pines to become a local hero sneaks into a bad gobbler's haunt at some point during the spring season. Ninety-nine percent of these hunters come at daybreak and from the same general direction—down a logging road, field edge, power-line cut, creek bottom or similar convenient access route.

From high in his tree each morning, a tough bird smiles all over himself as he patterns, both by sight and sound, the predictable moves of his adversaries. Unless a hunter blunders right beneath his tree, the turkey doesn't get all agitated and crash away. The crafty bird simply refuses to gobble and sails from his limb to an escape area located somewhere in his comfort zone.

Study every inch of a turkey's turf on aerial photos and topo maps. Then slip into his zone from different angles well before dawn each day. Step off a logging road or other well-traveled access lane, and ease over the backside of a ridge, slip up a ditch, pick your way through a pine thicket, etc.

FRESH APPROACHES TO A BAD TURKEY

Most hunters approach a bad turkey along a logging road, field edge or other convenient access route day after day. Patterning danger in these areas, the gobbler avoids them like the plague. Avoid traditional paths and walk the extra mile each morning—sneak up remote hollows, ease over the backsides of ridges and slip through stands of briars and pines. By varying your approaches and calling setups, you pique a bad turkey's interest. One day he's apt to fly down and strut over in search of a fresh hen in his domain.

Maneuvering in the dark woods, refrain from using a flashlight if possible. Going by moonlight, you will shuffle some leaves and brush, but that is okay. The turkey will take you for a deer or other nocturnal woods' traveler.

Resist the urge to owl hoot or crow call to a mean turkey who has been blasted with locator calling by other hunters all spring. Using an offbeat and subtle locating device, such as a hawk call or M.A.D.'s Dead Silence whistle, can sometimes make an old bird shock gobble and reveal his roost tree without revealing your presence in his zone. But in most cases, a silent and unobtrusive approach is best.

Slipping along, you may bust a few turkeys from their roosts. Hopefully these will be hens, which may sleep 100 yards or farther from your target gobbler. In the predawn darkness, a tom cannot determine what spooked his ladies. He might even think they are shifting around and "tree hopping" before fly-down time, something hens do more than most hunters imagine.

Actually, the more hens you push from a zone, the less calling competition you have when you finally set up to work a bad turkey. Hens begone is a positive thing!

Having penetrated a zone from a fresh direction, wait for the turkey to gobble on his own. Draw a line and try to slip within 100 yards his roost tree under cover of darkness before setting up to call.

Employing versatile approaches and setups each day keeps a bad gobbler on edge. You may eventually attract his interest with the yelping of a new hen in a fresh spot where the turkey feels comfortable strutting into your calls.

But even if a gobbler pulls the same old trick, clamming up on the ground and marching away, that is all right. Sit back in the glorious spring woods and let him do his thing.

Listen intently, trying to determine how many hens the gobbler has, and how long he consorts with them beneath his roost after flying down. Pinpoint his faint gobbles as he struts away. This patterning is all-important, for it helps you to determine the turkey's travel corridors to preferred strut zones. Use the daily information you glean to devise fresh approaches and setups on subsequent mornings.

Calling Bad Turkeys

To my mind, the key to coaxing a bad turkey is to use a variety of calling devices, as detailed in Chapter 3. Foremost, using box, slate and several styles of diaphragms, perhaps tossing in a few calls from a tube or wingbone, allows you to mimic multiple hens. The prospects of a ready-made harem lying in wait 100 yards or so from a gobbler's roost tree or strut zone is often enough to entice him your way, even if he's traveling with the same old gaggle of hens.

Remember what we said in Chapter 3 about gobblers becoming call-shy to one particular type of diaphragm call? Switching to a raspy box or high-pitched slate helps you break out of a calling rut created by other hunters who pepper an old bird with one popular style of mouth yelper day after day. Again, the prospect of a fresh hen in the area will often excite a mean gobbler and pull him in.

In most cases, a pressured turkey responds best to soft, "here and there" yelping, clucking and purring. Call just loudly enough so a gobbler can hear you. Use a cupped hand to throw your diaphragm yelping left and right. Reach behind you and cluck on a box or purr on a slate.

Moving around your soft calling can gain a gobbler's interest and keep him guessing as to the exact location of a hen playing hard to get. Often he cannot stand it. The bird may break strut and run in.

If a tough turkey shuns your subtle calling several mornings in a row, you have nothing to lose by giving him a good dose of aggressive yelping, cackling and cutting the next day. The optimum time to go call crazy is when you can set up within 100 yards or so of turkeys on the roost.

Call more than normal while a gobbler's hens are still in the trees. Cackle spiritedly to be the first hen on the ground, then back it up with excited yelping and cutting. This will definitely aggravate the hens and should excite the old tom.

The risk here is that a boss hen may fly down and take the gobbler away even

Many hunters hammer a bad turkey with one type of diaphragm calling morning after morning. By switching to a friction call with a unique tone, you pique a gobbler's interest. He may race in to check out the new hen in his breeding zone.

quicker than normal. Ah, but mature hens have pecking orders of their own, and often the leader of a hen pack feels the need to stroll over and check out a precocious new girl in town. She may bring a strutting gobbler in tow.

I've even had old gobblers break from their hens as they move away, and circle back to investigate my aggressive calling. This is the exception rather than the rule, but it's worth a try on occasion.

A technique as old as the hills, double-teaming has spelled doom for many a bad gobbler, especially those with few or no hens. Set up 100 yards or so from a turkey and have a buddy, preferably an adequate to expert caller, sit 30 to 50 yards behind you. As the caller moves around, yelping and scratching leaves to mimic a hen on the move, you remain silent and scan the understory. You just might spot the gobbler strutting in, trying to keep pace with what he perceives to be an aloof hen playing hard to get.

If a bad gobbler hits the ground and runs from your soft or aggressive calling several mornings in a row, try leaving him alone. Slip out of his zone and return at 10:00 or 11:00 a.m. Try to raise the turkey with sharp yelping or cutting. If the gobbler's hens have left him, he might respond to your calling. This tactic can be especially effective in late April or May when most mature hens are off laying and incubating eggs.

If you fail to strike a gobbler, relax and enjoy yourself. Set up in an oak flat, field edge or canyon bottom where you think a bad gobbler travels and struts during the day. Make a little brush blind, climb in, pull up your face mask, ready your shotgun across your knee and call softly and sparingly for a couple of hours.

If the turkey's working the area, he may or may not gobble at you. But listen for him drumming or shuffling leaves with his big feet. If the gobbler is lonely, he may pop up in front of your gun barrel when you least expect it. Many a wise old gobbler has lost his beard and spurs to patient turkey hunters using this simple yet sound technique.

If afternoon hunting is legal in your area, stick in a gobbler's zone right up until roosting time. Thirty minutes or so before fly-up, cackle excitedly like a hen going to the limb early. Then lay down your calls and wait.

A bad turkey may not answer your call, but the thought of roosting alongside a new hen may intrigue him enough to bring him your way. But even if this technique fails to produce, you can sit in the calm woods at dusk and listen for the wingbeats of turkeys flying up in the vicinity. If you hear the gobbler and his hens going to roost, you know where to begin the glorious if frustrating pursuit first thing the next morning.

Offbeat Tactics For Bad Birds

When going to war with a bad gobbler, you must dig as deeply as possible into your bag of tricks. Try not calling at all on occasion. Granted, this is difficult to do, for coaxing a gobbler to the call is the essence of spring turkey hunting.

To get a bad turkey thinking your way at dawn, gently tap and rub a tree with your wing to simulate a hen preening and turning on her limb.

Slip quietly into a gobbler's zone, set up in a potential travel lane or strut zone and simply scratch leaves to simulate turkeys walking and feeding in the midday woods.

Several years ago, my dad, Will Hanback, ran across a bad turkey on a hard-hunted tract of paper company land in Virginia. Dad set up and called to that gobbler for a week. The turkey would roar once or twice in the tree, fly down and gobble proudly again 300 yards away.

One morning around 11:00 o'clock, my father was easing down a logging road, going slow and listening. His feet shuffled some oak leaves—the turkey boomed a gobbled 70 yards away! Dad dived against an oak tree and scratched more leaves, but never yelped once. He shot the 18-pound Eastern with 1 1/4-inch spurs as it walked silently up in search of its leaf-shuffling brethren.

I always carry a hen wing in my vest and use it to simulate a turkey flying down at dawn. Several years ago in southern Mississippi, my friend Ron Jolly of Primos Calls showed me a unique twist when "winging it" for bad gobblers.

"Early in the morning, I like to tap a tree gently with my wing," Jolly whispered as we set up on a tough old bird with a bevy of hens. "It sounds like a hen moving around on the limb. I use it to get a gobbler's attention before calling. I want to get him thinking my way."

Set up 20 yards from Jolly, I could barely hear him scraping a pine tree. But almost every time he tapped and rubbed the wing against the bark, the turkey gobbled. As dawn broke and hens began yelping, we joined in with soft clucks, yelps and purrs. Thinking our way, the gobbler crashed down and strutted within 30 yards of me. I shot the 16-pound bird with inch-plus spurs as his hens pitched down in all directions.

Turkey decoys, if legal in your hunting area, can be powerful tools for duping bad gobblers. But a single hen decoy, which most hunters use, normally won't cut it. You should throw a fake jake into the mix.

A bad gobbler is a male chauvinist and a bully rolled up in one bundle of black feathers. Nine times out of 10, he will address a poor little jake before strutting over to a nearby hen, just to show off his macho image.

Allow a gobbler to bully his way into shotgun range by setting one or two hen decoys, along with a fake jake, 30 yards from your calling position. Good, safe strategy is to place the decoys along the edge of a field or in a mature hardwood flat where they can be easily seen and approached by an incoming gobbler. In these open areas, you can quickly spot and ward off a nitwit who may resort to the incredibly dangerous practice of stalking your decoys.

Play off a dominant gobbler's machismo by setting a fake jake near a hen decoy. When a bad turkey struts in to exude his dominance over the foam jake, you can turn the tables on him.

Summary

Use fresh approach angles and setups, vary your calling schemes from soft to aggressive, scratch leaves, tap a wing on a tree and set out a jake decoy. Experiment with a variety of solid and innovative strategies, and a wise old gobbler will still run you in circles most mornings. It is just the nature of these woodland legends.

But persevere and revel in the obsession, for sooner or later it will happen. It may take days, weeks or the better part of a spring season, but finally you'll trick the devil into shotgun range. When you sling a 16-pound gobbler with a pencil-thin beard over your shoulder and feel his needle-sharp hooks in the palm of your hand, you will feel an odd mix of elation and sadness. Glad to have won the war and achieved local hero status, yet a little blue knowing that bad turkey won't be out there to hunt any more.

I race quickly out to retrieve the gobblers I shoot. Some "dead" turkeys are lost because hunters fool around getting on them after the shot.

Chapter 13

The Final 40 Yards

You locate a gobbling turkey, maneuver in nicely and give him your sweetest calling. For once everything clicks. The old boy is coming, you hear him drumming intensely and shuffling leaves with his big pink feet. Seventy, 60, 50 yards. . . The moment of truth is upon you.

This is the most exhilarating phase of a spring turkey hunt. It is also when many golden opportunities are blown to shreds. Hunters freezing up, fidgeting around too much and exhibiting awful shotgun technique have allowed who knows how many gobblers to keep their long beards and sharp spurs intact over time.

In previous chapters, we focused on general calling positions for morning and midday hunts. Here, let's delve into the critical intricacies of setting up against trees and firing at toms. Heed this advice. How you perform during those frenzied seconds when gobblers close inside of 40 yards is what makes or breaks spring turkey hunts.

Setup Specifics

On most hunts, you should sit on the ground with your back planted firmly against a wide-trunked tree. This helps to break your outline and hide you from an incoming tom. It also provides the foundation for a rock-solid shooting position. Finally, backing up to a large tree provides safety and peace of mind should some reckless nitwit stalk either your yelping or the gobbling of the turkey you are working.

Owing to the terrain or the location of a roosted or strutting gobbler, finding a strategic setup tree is sometimes impossible. For example, I've yelped to Rio Grandes strutting in the south Texas brush country where the nearest live oak tree was a mile away. When chasing Merriam's turkeys in open canyons or Easterns around huge fields, burns or clearcuts, you may also find convenient setup trees in short supply.

When this is the case, back up against something—a rock, fallen log, shrub or pocket of brush. Often a cluster of mesquite, oak brush, greenbrier or other shrubbery can form a web-like back support that breaks your outline and solidifies your shooting station.

I have shot a few turkeys from the prone position over the years, lying over a ditch bank or similar rise in the terrain, boring my elbows into the earth to anchor my shotgun and poking its barrel through low-growing vegetation at gobblers strutting into range. Prone is steady to shoot from, but limits your visibility and your ability to maneuver your gun should a tom circle in to either side.

How you perform during those frenzied minutes when a gobbler closes in to your setup is what makes or breaks spring turkey hunts.

But sometimes flattening out in a field, prairie or other treeless area is the only way to set up where a gobbler feels comfortable drifting to your calls. So go prone when you must.

But let's return to the tree setup, for it is from this position that the vast majority of gobblers are fired upon. Whenever possible, I like to select a big tree that sits slightly above an open area where I believe a turkey will approach. Gaining an extra foot or two of elevation greatly increases your visibility as you scan the dense understory for incoming gobblers.

Conversely, many excellent turkey hunters I know like to hunker low against trees, feeling this positions them below the sight plane of sharp-eyed gobblers looking hard for calling hens. There is a lot of merit to this theory, but I still prefer the visibility advantage of slight elevation. If you prefer the extra concealment of a "scrunch" setup, stay low.

Before ever yelping to a gobbler, make your shooting station clean and comfortable. Use pruning shears to trim saplings, vines,

The ultimate setup: Back against a wide tree with your knees pulled up into your body. If you shoot right-handed, level your shotgun across your left knee (vice versa for southpaws).

briars or thorns that might poke your back, rump, legs, arms or head. Clip away any inhospitable stuff that might cause you to squirm around and spook a turkey.

More importantly, trim any saplings, low-growing limbs or brush that might impede the smooth swing of your shotgun barrel. Always strive to set up where you can fluidly cover an 180-degree arc out front of your tree, because you never know precisely where a gobbler's white-capped head will pop up in the green foliage.

I rarely take the time to build a blind around my setup tree, though I know many successful hunters who do. If you can do it quickly and with minimal noise and movement, assembling a camouflage mesh blind undoubtedly helps to turn you invisible.

Some turkey hunting friends of mine craft little calling hides out of rotting branches and green-leaf saplings. Again, I normally don't go to all that trouble, but I sometimes clip a few leafy branches and stake them well out in front of my gun barrel. This helps to break my outline, especially when the dormant woods are wide-open in early spring.

A low-profile setup against a fallen log, rock, patch of brush or other available cover can be effective.

As you prepare to go to war with a gobbler, lay tube, box and slate calls, along with necessary sandpaper and chalk, within easy reach on the ground beside you. This keeps you from rifling through your vest, and hence minimizes movement, as you sweet-talk a nearby gobbler with a variety of calling devices.

It is now time to put the vital finishing touches on your setup. If you shoot right-handed, twist into a tree so that your left shoulder points in the direction you think the gobbler will appear (vice versa for lefties). This allows you to cover a wide frontal arc with minimal shotgun movement.

Pull your knees tightly up into your body. A right-hander should lay his gun firmly across his left knee (vice versa for southpaws). Keep your shotgun up, leveled and ready for action as you call to a turkey.

Scan the turf before you to determine primary and secondary shooting lanes in the ground foliage. Mentally estimate the range to large rocks, fallen trees, stumps and other prominent markers within 40 yards of your setup. If and when a gobbler steps alongside one of these landmarks, you subconsciously know he is within shotgun range.

Flow With A Gobbler

Point your shotgun in front of you and freeze. Don't blink an eye or move a muscle. Sound familiar? Probably, because over the years spring turkey hunters have been cautioned to sit like stones as sharp-eyed gobblers work to their calls.

I believe that freezing up is one of the gravest mistakes a hunter can make! You become so tentative and frightened of busting a turkey that you sit like a knot on a log and allow the bird to strut in to a place where he is virtually impossible to kill.

Locked down, you may be forced to let a longbeard walk off. And if he does, chances are you will never call him back again. The turkey came to that spot once, but didn't find the calling hen he was pining for. He will be leery to return.

Worse, you might have to swing your shotgun frantically and take an off-balance shot at a gobbler that angles in to your setup. Lots of turkeys are missed or crippled this way.

The best advice I can give you is to flow with a gobbler who commits to your calls. Obviously you cannot move wildly, body weaving around a tree, whipping your head from side to side or waving your

Whenever possible, set up on a little point of ground that affords a foot or two of extra visibility. Note how this hunter is twisting around his setup tree, flowing with a gobbler as he approaches.

shotgun barrel like a magic wand. But you must move a little bit, synchronizing with a turkey as he waltzes in. So doing, you can ease slowly and fluidly into final position where you can kill an approaching tom quickly, cleanly and confidently with one shot.

Begin fine-tuning your shooting form before ever laying eyes on a gobbler you are working. Each time a turkey standing hidden in the foliage 60 to 75 yards out cuts loose a gobble, shift your coiled body and shotgun in his direction. Continue flowing with the subtle sounds of a bird drumming, shuffling leaves with his feet or popping his wings against brush. Don't make any abrupt, foolish moves, just ease around fluidly. It is easier than you might imagine to pivot your body and gun barrel a full 180 degrees as a gobbler circles in.

Closing the Sale

Upon spotting an incoming bird, take a deep breath to calm your nerves and still your racing heart. A long-bearded gobbler doing the herky-jerky as he walks in, craning his long, red periscope to look for a hen, exploding into sun-drenched strut and then dropping his fan to gobble lustily in your face, can cause even the most seasoned turkey hunter to turn to mush.

Look long and hard to identify the bird as a dominant gobbler. As mentioned many times in this book, fringe turkeys tag along with boss gobblers more than ever today. It is common for a small, drab-brown hen or a brush-bearded jake to run in to your calls before a mature gobbler can get there.

Focus on a mature tom's kaleidoscopic head. Generally in the spring it will appear as big and as white as a softball, but it may pulse to cherry red to Carolina blue before your eyes. Scour the understory for a long beard curving like a sickle from a tom's shiny black chest.

If a turkey struts before your eyes, which he may well do, examine his fan. A mature gobbler's 18 tail feathers are perfectly even in length, while a jake's middle tail rectrices are noticeably longer than the sides of his fan.

Again, don't be petrified to move if necessary to align your shotgun barrel on a gobbler's head and neck vitals. Cutting your eyes inside a camouflage face mask will never spook a tom, so keep him in sight at all times. (Wild turkeys are sharp for sure, but do not possess the mystical powers many hunters attribute to them!) When a gobbler's head ducks behind a tree, rock, fallen log or pocket of brush, ease your shotgun smoothly but quickly to cover an opening where he should reappear.

And remember this: A jittery old tom will sometimes freeze behind an obstacle, then curl his warty head back to peer inquisitively in your direction. I think this is the wild turkey's variation of the white-tailed deer's head bob. Whatever the case, the fact remains that if you move too tentatively, a gobbler might look back and bust you.

A fine time to align your gun barrel is when a strutting gobbler turns directly away from you, his head obscured by his great fan.

An excellent time to fine-tune your shotgun alignment is when a gobbler's head is obscured by his great fan. (Photo courtesy Perfection Turkey Calls)

Again, cover the bird the quickly. An old turkey who is prone to drop strut and look around for danger seems to have eyes in the back of his crinkly head. Even if he appears to be looking away, he will bust you if you tarry and wave your gun barrel around.

Always look for ground foliage between you and a gobbler, something many hunters forget to do in the heat of battle. You'll have to shoot through some stuff most of the time, but search for inch-thick limbs and saplings that can destroy your shot pattern and break your heart.

One morning in Virginia years ago, I called "The Lion" (aptly named for his loud, roaring gobble) within 35 yards. I flowed with the turkey, positioned my shotgun's barrel beads perfectly on his neck, pressed the trigger and watched in horror as the huge tom ducked his head and flashed away, completely unscathed.

Each time I miss a gobbler (anyone who tells you he never misses has either never hunted turkeys much or is lying through his teeth), I investigate the crime scene. I walked out to where The Lion had stood in all his gaudy splendor, knelt down and looked back to my setup tree along the path where my shot pattern had flown.

You'll have to shoot through some ground foliage most of the time, but always check for thick limbs and saplings between you and a gobbler. Shift your shotgun to take any pattern-busting obstacles out of play before firing. (Photo courtesy Perfection Turkey Calls)

This miss was a no-brainer. A thick, heavily limbed oak sapling that I had failed to see and consider was toppled over and blown to shreds. I counted 20 pellet holes in the obstruction, and who knows how many fliers it had created. Unlucky for me but fortunate for The Lion, who I really educated that day. He played the game and roared at my calls for the remainder of the season, yet I never glimpsed him again.

Having checked for pattern-busting obstacles and shifted your shotgun slightly to take them out of play if necessary, wait for gobblers to close within 40 yards before thinking of firing. No doubt that modern 12-gauge shotguns and three- or 3 1/2-inch magnum loads can drop turkeys cleanly out to 60 yards. But there is a lot of luck involved in those long-range shots.

Beyond 40 paces, aligning a shotgun's front barrel bead on a turkey's head/neck vitals is pretty much a guessing game. The bead blots out most of the turkey (granted, a low-magnification scope can help to alleviate this problem). But still, it is hard to tell what a shot pattern fired from a scoped or open-sighted shotgun is doing as it clips limbs, branches and brush out to 45 yards and beyond. Long shots are just too risky.

Whenever possible, I like to let a gobbler slip within 35 yards, reveling in his wild beauty and aura before firing. If the tom is willing to come within 30 or 25 yards, all the better. But don't let him walk inside 20 yards, where your pattern of buffered, copper-plated 4s, 5s or 6s is no larger than a tennis ball.

Also, a gobbler has an uncanny ability to pick you out of the cover at extremely close range, no matter how well camouflaged and hidden you are. And a skittish turkey at 15 to 20 yards will often all at once sense that something is amiss when he fails to see a calling hen, causing him to duck his head and bolt before you can bang off a close-range shot.

When a turkey pops into strut, curling his neck back into his body and largely obscuring his neck vertebrae, hold your fire. I have killed a few gobblers in dead strut because they were close, all within 25 yards, and I figured that would be the only shot I would get in those particular situations. But it is always best to break a gobbler out of strut by clucking on a mouth diaphragm.

Contrary to what you might have been taught years ago, never aim solely for a gobbler's head. For starters, the top half of your shot

This big gobbler offers the perfect target — periscope extended and head turned sideways. Cheek your shotgun and aim just above the major caruncles, the big, fleshy lobes at the base of the tom's neck. (Photo courtesy Perfection Turkey Calls)

pattern will be useless, collecting only air. And if a jittery turkey turns, dips or jerks his head, something he is prone to do as he paces nervously around looking for the calling hen, you'll miss clean as a whistle.

When a gobbler runs his neck up like a periscope to look for the clucking hen, dig your cheek firmly into your shotgun's stock. I mean really cheek that gun! Most turkey misses can be attributed to hunters failing to get face down into their gunstocks. If you unwittingly watch a gobbler over the top of your shotgun barrel as you depress the trigger, you will in all likelihood pull the shot high.

Center the barrel's front bead or blade (or the crosshairs of a scope) on the lower third of a turkey's neck. I like to aim just above the major caruncles, those large, fleshy, gaudy red bubbles that adorn the base of a gobbler's neck.

If possible, wait for a turkey to turn his head and neck sideways to you before firing. This is generally not a problem, as incoming toms twist their heads in all directions as they search for calling hens. A mature tom's head measures about five inches from beak to back of head. Face on, a gobbler's noggin is half that size. A turkey's broadside head and neck are easiest to align a shotgun bead on.

A disclaimer here: If a gobbler acts spooky and you think a head-on shot is all you will get, by all means go ahead and take him. Waiting for a tom to turn his head sideways offers the optimum sighting target, but you can kill him just as cleanly when he faces you if your shooting technique is otherwise solid.

Don't bang off the safety, especially those tight ones located on the trigger guard of many shotguns. Slowly reach under the shotgun's pistol grip and use the thumb and forefinger of your shooting hand to cushion the safety release. I suspect many a gobbler has been sent ducking through the foliage by the ill-timed metallic clicks of safeties.

Wait until the shot looks and feels just right, but if the gobbler alarm putts, you must fire immediately if you have a good opportunity. Sensing trouble because he has picked you out or has not seen a precocious hen, the turkey is fixing to duck his head and leave in a big hurry.

When the moment of truth finally arrives, press the shotgun's trigger as if you were shooting your centerfire deer rifle. Jerk the trigger and you may pull the shot high.

Race to a flopping bird, handling your shotgun carefully with its safety back on. Countless "dead" gobblers have been lost because hunters fooled around getting on them.

Get on a bird fast, but keep away from his flailing spurs. A gobbler will get the last lick in if you let him.

You can perform the age-old ritual of placing your boot on a fallen turkey's neck if you desire, but most of the time this is unnecessary if your shot was true. To preserve a gobbler's magnificent feathers for photographs, something I advise all hunters to do, press down on his flapping wings with gloved hands. But keep away from those flailing sharp spurs, which can seriously slash you. An old tom will get the last lick in if you let him, that I can tell you from experience.

Zipping an arrow through a jittery, sharp-eyed wild turkey in the spring woods near home is the ultimate challenge.

Chapter 14

The Archery Challenge

The gobbler paused in the oak flat and exploded into strut. His transformation was magnificent. Once sleek and black as coal in the new morning sun, the turkey was now a medicine ball of quivering and gaudy feathers.

My long-bearded quarry took three quick baby steps, then stopped and drooped his enormous white-barred wings. *Pfftt, duuummm, pfftt, duuummm.* His head flashed from red to blue to white as he drummed his subtle love tunes.

The turkey began spinning, posturing in all directions like a cocky male model working the runway at a fashion show. At once his coppery fan covered his pulsing head, and I maneuvered my weapon into shooting position.

In one silky motion, I raised the bow, angled it left and pulled the string. Wild turkeys seem to have eyes in the back of their crinkly heads, so I was not surprised the gobbler detected some movement. He dropped into half-strut, not really sure what he had seen. I placed the 25-yard pin on his upper back and released the arrow.

The aluminum projectile sizzled through the still morning air, frozen in flight for what seemed an eternity. It then clanged into a tree an inch over the turkey's back. He jumped four feet left and stared curiously at me before putt, putt, putting away.

I wanted to stomp around and cuss with that glazed, incredulous look on my face, the way you do when you miss a "sure" turkey with a shotgun and a charge of copper-plated 4s. But then I remembered this was bowhunting. I smiled and walked out to look for my arrow.

I have been fortunate enough to hunt most species of North American big game over the past two decades. Sheep, goats and grizzly bears in Alaska, elk and mule deer in western states, big-racked whitetails in Saskatchewan and many other places. All these animals, tough and clever in their own way, inhabit some of the wildest country left on earth. Having said all that, I believe that trying to zip an arrow through a jittery, sharp-eyed, 18-pound gobbler in the spring woods near home is possibly the grandest challenge in hunting.

Archery hunting for spring gobblers is booming in popularity across the country. I think it is because so many wild turkeys roam our fields and forests today. A hunter becomes skilled enough to nail a longbeard or two with his 12 gauge each season. Looking for a new level of excitement and challenge, he decides to carry a stick and string. He gets more than he bargained for and then some.

Before we delve into the specifics of bowhunting for spring toms, let me say that the sport is not for the faint of heart. You will spook a ton of turkeys as you set up and draw. You will loose many arrows. You will become frustrated, thinking the game is impossible. Then one day everything clicks, and you finally draw gobbler feathers. As you race out to claim your prize, you will cut loose a war scream never before heard in the spring turkey woods!

Bow Tackle For Gobblers

Your deer hunting bow and arrows will work just fine for turkeys. I shoot either a PSE Infinity or a Golden Eagle Hawk System that wears an overdraw and a multi-pin sight. With either of these bows, lightweight 2213 aluminum shafts fly well for me. These rigs are quiet and flat-shooting—two factors you need when hunting skittish longbeards with a penchant for jumping the string.

If you shoot a 65- to 70-pound bow for deer, you might consider lowering its draw weight to 50 or 55 pounds when spring gobbler hunting. This will enable you to pull and hold smoothly as a tom approaches. If you shoot a modern compound with a 65% or even 80% let-off, no problem. You can hold draw for extended periods while waiting for a good, clear shot at a turkey.

Use sharp, 100- or 125-grain broadheads (again, the same ones you shoot at whitetails) backed up with spring stoppers. Stoppers, which attach to shafts just behind broadheads, keep arrows from passing through gobblers. This helps to anchor flopping birds on the ground, and slows down the flight of toms that might take wing after the shot.

Wear head-to-toe camouflage, including gloves and face mask or paint as outlined in Chapter 2. If your bow does not wear a factory Trebark, Mossy Oak or Realtree finish, cover it with camouflage tape. And remember to conceal brightly fletched arrows in your quiver with a piece of camo cloth, or remove the quiver from your bow when you set up to call a turkey.

The Archery Setup

As when hunting with a shotgun, slip within 100 to 125 yards of a gobbling turkey whenever possible. Set up against a tree, fallen log, patch of brush or similar cover to break your outline. Put some foliage or brush in front of you, but be certain it will not impede the smooth swing, draw and release of your bow.

Set up with cover to break your outline. Be sure you have a couple of clear shooting lanes out front. Drawing and releasing arrows from the kneeling position is best on most spring gobbler hunts.

The next point is critical. Scan the ground foliage to make sure you have at least two wide-open shooting lanes out to 25 yards. A loosed arrow that strikes even a tiny sapling or limb will wobble harmlessly off course. If you can determine no brush-free shooting zones at a setup, relocate quickly, regardless of how close a turkey is and how hotly he might be gobbling. It is not only frustrating but foolhardy to call a tom to a spot where you cannot loose an accurate arrow at him.

A portable camouflage blind (see Chapter 2) that is quick and easy to set up is excellent for bowhunting gobblers. It will cover your movements as you work a box or slate and then lay down your friction call to pick up your bow. More importantly, a blind provides maximum concealment as you draw arrows. Choose a hide with ample width, as you may need to synchronize 180 degrees with an incoming gobbler.

Kneeling in a blind provides the most comfortable and solid bow-shooting platform. Shoot hundreds of practice arrows from the kneeling position before spring gobbler season opens. Most archers are accustomed to firing from the standing posture, either on the ground or in a tree stand. It takes lots of practice from kneeling to get a smooth draw and a comfortable sight picture down pat.

Bowhunting from a portable blind is excellent strategy. The camouflage mesh covers your moves as you lean up, draw your bow and let fly an arrow at a keen-eyed gobbler.

Actually, you may be able to bowhunt from the standing position on occasion. I once shot a gobbler while standing amid the uppermost limbs and leaves of a half-rotten oak tree recently toppled by high winds. I used my pruning shears to clip out an unencumbered shooting station. Such a "treetop" setup is excellent if you can find one positioned strategically in the vicinity of a gobbling turkey.

You can also try standing behind a large tree. Stay hidden behind the tree as you draw your bow, then lean out slightly left or right to loose an arrow as a gobbler approaches. On the surface, this seems to be the ultimate setup. Problem is, six feet of you (give or take a few inches) is leaning out smack in the middle of a gobbler's sight plane. All things considered, you are probably best off assuming the kneeling position on most bowhunts.

An archer should definitely master several diaphragm calls with various tones and rasp. You can use a box or slate call when a turkey is out there 75 to 100 yards. But when he starts moving in, switch to diaphragms. By interchanging mouth yelpers, you can run a full range of raspy to high-pitched yelps and clucks while holding your bow upright and ready.

By far, the most effective way to bowhunt turkeys is to pull the old double-team trick. Have a partner set up and call behind you. A

Archers should master several types of diaphragm calls. This allows you to keep your bow upright and ready while calling spiritedly to approaching toms.

gobbler will often strut unsuspectingly into bow range as he rivets his attention on your buddy's clucks, yelps and purrs.

Archery hunting with a partner or solo, try a decoy if legal in your area. Set a foam hen in a clear shooting lane 15 to 20 yards from your setup. Make sure it can twirl in the breeze for added realism.

If a gobbler struts in and displays in all his gaudy splendor for your fake, he may not notice the movement as you lean up and draw an arrow. Also, a decoy helps you pinpoint the range to a turkey, which is critical when bowhunting. If a tom stands alongside your fake hen, you know to use either the 15- or 20-yard sight pin. If he struts several steps behind your decoy, move to the 25-yard pin. Conversely, if the turkey parades in front of your decoy, you know you need to either hold low with the 20-yard pin or switch to a 10-yard sight if you have one.

Making the Shot

First, identify the incoming bird to be a gobbler. Look for a big, color-pulsing head and a beard—short or long.

All of the tactical advice mentioned thus far in this book pertains to the pursuit of long-bearded, sharp-spurred gobblers with a shotgun. When archery hunting, arrowing a mature tom with a nine-inch beard and inch-plus hooks should be your goal. But I would not pass up a jake with a four-inch beard, especially if you have never killed a wild turkey with your bow. Any gobbler taken with a stick and string is a trophy to be proud of.

Drawing an arrow on a spooky, sharp-eyed turkey is the most difficult task you will ever face in the spring woods. Pull the bow string only when a gobbler's head dips behind a tree, rock, fallen log or patch of brush. An excellent time to draw is when a strutting tom's head is obscured by his tail fan.

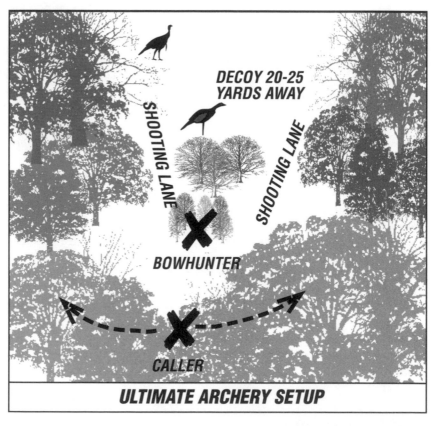

Here's the ultimate bowhunting setup: A foam hen decoy staked in an opening and twirling in the breeze. Ample cover in front of the archer to break his outline and hide his movements. In the background, a partner float calling and scratching leaves to direct an incoming gobbler's attention away from the bowhunter as he draws and fires an arrow through one of two wide-open shooting lanes.

As mentioned, turkeys are notorious string jumpers, so let them close to within 25 yards before releasing an arrow. Fifteen- to 20-yard shots are better yet. Remember to look closely for any shaft-deflecting saplings, limbs and brush that will ruin a hunt.

Unless you can shoot a bow like William Tell, aim not for a gobbler's head and neck, as you would when shotgun hunting, but for his body vitals. If a tom is facing you, hold on his upper chest. Center on a gobbler's upper back when he turns directly away. When a turkey goes broadside, place your sight pin on the base of his great wing.

Whatever the case, hold steady, say a little prayer and send the arrow smoothly on its way. If you strike feathers, bust out of your blind immediately. You may have to run down a flopping bird. If the gobbler takes wing, run after him and scan the skyline, hoping to see him fall. Pause and listen for the tom to thump heavily to the ground, then get on him quickly.

This is definitely the time to place your boot upon the neck of a flopping gobbler, hold your bow high in the sky and cut loose a whoop for all the world to hear. Having met the ultimate challenge in spring turkey hunting, you passed with flying colors.

Boating for gobblers is most practical if a large federal forest or state wildlife management area borders lakes, rivers or streams in your region.

Chapter 15

Boating For Longbeards

A couple of winters ago, Mark Drury called me up and said, "Let's go boat hunt some turkeys this spring."

The call maker's offer had the shocking power of a hen cutt to a two-year-old gobbler. "I'm in!" I roared into the telephone. Locked in an office in January, peering out the window at a landscape that has the look and feel of frozen aluminum, a work- weary turkey addict pines for those warm, green spring days when he can play hooky again. In this case, the prospect of chasing the king of game birds from a bass boat, something I had never done before, made the tag end of winter zoom by.

Before I knew it, Mark, his brother, Terry, and I were motoring across a Midwestern lake in a sleek Ranger boat one April evening, a warm breeze whipping our faces and the anticipation of the next dawn's hunt firing our souls. We swung the bass craft into a secluded cove and cut the inboard.

"Listen to this," Mark smiled. He owl hooted, and a turkey bellowed, his gobble rolling like a jolt of thunder across the glassy water.

We cranked the engine, and I swear the turkey gobbled at it! "Don't worry," Mark read my mind. "He'll still be there in the morning."

We motored into four other coves that evening and repeated the locating scenario, hooting and cutting on slate calls to shock gobbles from six other lovesick toms. With binoculars we zeroed in on three gobblers roosted near shore, their long- bearded silhouettes etched against the crimson sunset. The turkeys could plainly see us floating around out there in our boat, yet they paid us little attention, just watching and honoring us with their wonderful gobbles. I found that amazing.

In pitch-black darkness the next morning, we beached our vessel and climbed a ridge to the first turkey who had treated us to a chorus of gravelly shock gobbling the previous evening. Not surprisingly, the old tom was roosted with a bevy of hens and shunned our calling. No problem. We raced back to the boat, fired the engine and blasted off for another cove where we had put to bed a pair of gobblers.

As our red-and-silver Ranger planed out across the water, we spotted a beautiful Eastern monarch strutting on the open, sandy lake shore for all the world to see. All puffed up in his gaudy display for hens, the turkey never glanced our way as we motored past at 150 yards.

"These gobblers are used to fishing boats zipping past them each day," Mark said. "As long as they don't see you stop the boat and get out, they pay you no mind." Used to playing the ultimate conceal-ment game, I was thunderstruck by that little tidbit of information.

At 10:00 a.m. we glassed a pair of longbeards drifting up the sandy lake shore and into a point of hardwood timber. We cut the engine and drifted into a nearby cove. After walking all of 100 yards into woods, we cutt on box calls. Not two but three gobblers roared up the hollow.

Mark and I set up against trees while Terry positioned his video camera behind us. We gave Terry the thumbs-up, and he floated out a couple of seductive yelps. The pair of gobblers, no doubt brothers, bellowed 100 yards to my left. Terry's camera was whirring now. He was confident the turkeys were coming, and I was too.

Two white heads, brilliant as balls of polished ivory in the mid-morning sunshine, bobbed in the green foliage. Mark and I wanted to double, but the toms strutted in fast to my side. I rolled the lead longbeard at 20 yards. Terry expertly captured the action for use on the Drury boys' *Spur Of The Moment* video.

Using our bass boat to access miles of remote country teeming with turkeys, the three of us limited out on long-bearded Easterns in three days of scintillating hunting. This on well-used public land! You, too, can experience similar fun and success by boating for gobblers.

Where and How to Boat Hunt

The boating option is most practical if a state wildlife manage-ment area, national forest or other public tract with a healthy turkey population borders lakes, rivers or streams in your region. If a water source is rimmed by private property, you must obtain hunting per-mission from the appropriate landowners before setting out on a floating adventure.

Obtain topographical maps and aerial photographs of the hunt-able ground surrounding lakes, rivers and streams. Check the charts for out-of-the-way coves, creek mouths and backwaters

The Drurys and I used a sleek, fast Ranger to cover a big lake on our Mid-western turkey hunt. Tailor your vessel—bass boat, aluminum johnboat or canoe—to the size of the water you float-hunt.

A boat allows you to access secluded lake coves in the evening. After cutting the motor, hen cutt, crow call or owl hoot to locate roosted gobblers for the next morning's hunt.

rimmed with mixed pine-hardwood forests, oak hollows and ridges, field edges, and similar prime turkey habitat. Areas inaccessible from roads but easily reached by boat typically provide the best spring gobbler hunting.

To hunt safely and efficiently, tailor your choice of vessel to the water source you plan to hunt. On my Midwestern trip with the Drurys, our powerful bass boat allowed us to swiftly cover miles of water as we prospected the wooded fringes for gobblers. In the past, Mark and Terry had successfully used an aluminum john boat and outboard on the same big lake, though they noted this slowed down their turkey scouting and locating time.

A 17-foot canoe is perfect for floating the countless small rivers and streams that wend through Eastern turkey range. Choose an ABS-plastic model that slips easily over riffles and rocks and allows you to float-hunt quietly.

Before a spring season opens, motor around a lake or paddle down a river or stream. Beach your vessel frequently to scout for fresh turkey tracks, droppings and scratchings. Secluded and open lake shores and sandbars along waterways are prime strutting areas for toms, so look for the intriguing sign where their primary wings scuffed the ground.

After beaching your craft, you can hike into prime turkey habitats inaccessible to foot hunters. That is often where you will find unpressured gobblers talking.

Scout a couple of days to get a good feel for the new hunting area. From your boat, try to locate several gobbling turkeys at dusk. This will allow you to paddle or motor in safely and efficiently in the dark come opening morning.

A final note: It is incredibly unethical and dangerous to try to shoot at a strutting gobbler from a boat, especially one powered by a motor. It is also illegal in most states. Carry an unloaded shotgun in a floatable soft case as you access your hunting ground. After beaching your boat or canoe, load up and experience some intriguing turkey hunting.

Canoe-Hopping for Gobblers

One spring, call maker David Hale and I hunted at Tara Lodge near Vicksburg, Mississippi. Now Tara is home to a healthy population of Eastern wild turkeys, but it just so happened that the timing of our hunt was not so hot. The second phase of peak gobbling was days away, and few henned-up toms were hammering it from their limbs.

But our guide for the hunt, Brad Farris, knew where a couple of lonely longbeards were gobbling—on a narrow island surrounded by deep backwaters. When you turkey hunt in the Mississippi Delta and many other places in the Deep South, you are at the whims of the water levels.

"Brad, we need to hunt those turkeys," Hale said. I nodded in full agreement.

"No problem," said Brad, a quiet and amiable guy. "I've got a canoe down by one edge of the water. We'll just hop over there to 'em."

In heavy darkness the next morning, the three of us piled into the plastic canoe. Brad paddled, I held my unloaded Mossberg and Hale cradled his expensive video camera like his firstborn. After floating a good 50 yards, the bow of the canoe slid onto dry ground. Then the turkey roared.

Lo and behold, the water-loving warrior was roosted across another backwater! We contemplated portaging our canoe across the island and putting in again, but we figured the old devil would see us in the growing light.

Brad offered that we should set up and call in hopes the gobbler would sail over to us. Delta turkeys are used to flying across water every day, so I thought this was a good game plan.

The turkey flew down and lockjaw set in. "Hens," I whispered to Hale. "You can take that to the bank," my Kentucky friend sparred back.

For an hour we sat calling and whispering and enjoying the grand spring morning, then decided to walk out an old logging trail and try to cutt up another tom. Halfway into our stroll, Hale hissed, "Get down." Like three battle-ready marines, we hit the dirt as a hen stepped out into the road 125 yards away.

Mississippi guide Brad Farris (right) and I canoed all of 50 yards across a backwater to hunt this long-bearded, sharp-spurred Eastern. Sometimes "boat hopping" is the only way to access gobbling turkeys.

We crawled back and around a little bend. Brad staked out a decoy while I searched anxiously for a shooting spot, finally lying prone over a ditch bank where I could see a good stretch of the turkey highway. If there was a gobbler running with the hen, he would have to round the curve to investigate our calling. This would put him precisely 20 yards in front of my shotgun barrel.

Hale set up 10 yards behind me and anchored his video camera on a tripod. Without warning a turkey boomed a lusty gobble down the road bed. Hale yelped softly, and I heard his camera whir to life. Had a Delta gobbler fallen into our laps?

No, three of them had. Our little hen friend pecked past me at 10 yards. Frozen like a brass statue, I prayed for her to hurry up and feed on by because I needed to ease my shotgun a foot to the right to align on one of three magnificent road warriors strutting and drumming and fixing to run me over.

The hen passed and I entered turkey hunting dream land— positioned between three huge longbeards and their old boss mate. Hale clucked, my signal that he had the gobblers in his camera's viewfinder and time to shoot. The shotgun roared on the island, and a 17-pound gobbler with an 11-inch beard and 1 1/4-inch spurs thundered to the ground.

The moral of this story: Sometimes you don't have to plan an elaborate float hunt with a gleaming bass boat to have success. Often, just using a canoe or a johnboat to skip across a deep stream, swamp or backwater can give you a gigantic edge.

If you hunt around water, try boat-hopping to access secluded islands and peninsulas where turkeys, especially old long-spurred gobblers, love to roost and strut. On public lands, this puts distance between you and the other hunters on foot, allowing you to find and call to unpressured toms. And even if you hunt private ground, a boat or canoe can often carry you to the only gobbling turkeys in the county.

Most spring turkey hunters bag an Eastern longbeard first, then flirt with the idea of embarking on a grand slam. The pursuit of the three remaining races of gobblers is more practical and affordable than you might imagine.

Chapter 16

Quest For A Grand Slam

You begin by chasing whichever subspecies of wild turkey is found on public or private land near home. You go at it hard and with zest, honing your woodsmanship and calling skills over time. Soon, you can take a long-bearded gobbler or two most every spring with relative ease. A good hunter who is now thoroughly addicted to the spring pursuit, you start to wonder, "What would it be like to broaden my turkey hunting horizons?"

You have been struck, my friend, with grand slam fever, the uncontrollable urge to bag a mature gobbler from each of the four huntable strains of American wild turkeys. The question now becomes, "Is a slam in the cards for me, a turkey hunter of average means and vacation time?"

To that I answer a resounding, "Yes!" What follows is your guide to planning fun, affordable and quality spring gobbler hunts across the United States.

Targeting Turkey States

The vast majority of spring turkey hunters live in proximity to the Eastern subspecies, the most abundant and widespread wild turkey in the country. An estimated 2.6 million to 3 million Easterns inhabit hardwood forests from the Atlantic Coast to the eastern portions of Texas, Kansas and Minnesota.

Makes sense, then, that most hunters embark on their quest for a grand slam by chasing Easterns near home, or perhaps by traveling to hunt the birds in a neighboring state. Sharpen your skills on crafty Eastern longbeards, and you're primed to hunt the three remaining races of gobblers.

Westerners and Floridians can travel to hunt the Eastern subspecies in more than 35 states. If you're coming from out West, it makes sense to target states on the westernmost fringe of the

Eastern's range. The logistics will be easy to plan and the second leg of your slam will be most affordable.

Missouri, with an estimated 400,000 turkeys in good brood-production years, is an excellent place to hunt Easterns. The Show Me State's notoriously hard-gobbling toms often tip the scales at 25 pounds, offering yet another element of intrigue to the quest.

Iowa and Arkansas, with more than 100,000 turkeys apiece, are good spots to chase Easterns. And you can never go wrong by venturing across the Mississippi River (or north if you live in south Florida) to call the wildest of all turkeys in their ancestral Southern range. Mississippi, Alabama and Georgia each have 300,000 to 400,000 Eastern turkeys most springs.

Other states with healthy populations of Easterns include Pennsylvania (175,000 birds), Virginia (95,000 turkeys), West Virginia and South Carolina (80,000 birds apiece) and Wisconsin (60,000 birds). I recently hunted in Illinois, an up-and-coming hot spot with 35,000 Easterns, and heard a ton of gobbling.

Most slam-seeking hunters target Texas for a crack at the Rio Grande subspecies, and for good reason. With an estimated 600,000 to 700,000 birds in strong brood-production years, Texas is home to 85 percent of the Rio Grande population in the United States. Good hunting can also be found in Oklahoma and Kansas, where 40,000 to 60,000 Rios roam the central and western portions of each state.

Some 200,000 Merriam's, which I consider to be the most beautiful wild turkeys of all, inhabit 15 Western states. I've shot the iridescent gobblers with blond-tipped tail coverts and fans in the ponderosa pines of South Dakota and the arid high country of New Mexico. Each state, with an estimated 30,000 birds, is a popular and productive destination for traveling turkey hunters.

Home to an estimated 80,000 Merriam's, eastern Montana is an often overlooked but dynamite place to spring hunt. With 20,000 turkeys, eastern Wyoming is a good bet as well.

You must beeline south to the land of sun and fun to hunt the Osceola, or Florida, subspecies. With a restricted range and population (estimated at 100,000 birds), the Osceola is the most prized wild turkey of all, typically the capstone of a hunter's grand slam.

Pull out a road map and draw a line from Jacksonville to the mouth of the Suwannee River in western Florida. Go south of this demarcation line for a true Osceola like the Seminole Indians hunted in a bygone era. Gobblers taken in northern Florida are classified as Easterns or Eastern/Osceola hybrids.

Pinpointing Gobbler Zones

Targeting top turkey states builds a solid foundation for planning a grand slam, but used alone this information can be misleading. For example, you may assume that you can head anywhere in Texas and yelp in a Rio Grande gobbler. Not so. Dense populations of Rios are found in the central and southern portions of the state, but many eastern and western counties are devoid of wild turkeys.

Well in advance of a journey, research your target states to pinpoint hot gobbler zones. Contact the wildlife agency of each state you plan to visit. Obtain current regulations and turkey-permit applications if needed. Some states, such as Arizona, Iowa, Illinois and Florida, hold drawings for turkey tags in certain areas.

Call or write state wild turkey biologists. Ask them about turkey densities, recent brood production and spring hunting forecasts for various regions and counties. Strive to hunt areas with 16 to more than 25 turkeys per section, but be advised that excellent hunting can be found in pockets with fewer birds.

For a crack at a Merriam's gobbler, you can camp on public land or fee hunt ranches from South Dakota to New Mexico. Many western lodges also cater to traveling turkey hunters.

Ask biologists when periods of peak gobbling typically occur in various regions. As mentioned in Chapter 1, planning a hunt when hard-gobbling toms gather hens early in the season, or when hens leave lonely gobblers to nest late in the spring, adds zest to the quest and dramatically increases your odds of success.

Public Land Hunts

Calling in 20 states over the past two decades, I've experienced some excellent spring gobbler hunting on federally managed lands.

States with the most National Forest acreage in Eastern turkey range include Virginia, West Virginia, Arkansas and Missouri. Smaller tracts of federal forests are scattered over many Eastern, Southern and Midwestern states.

The 1.2 million-acre Black Hills National Forest in western South Dakota and eastern Wyoming is a premier place to hunt Merriam's. You can also chase the beautiful turkeys in national forests in Arizona and New Mexico, and on Bureau of Land Management (BLM) acreage in eastern Montana.

Many state wildlife management areas offer fair to good spring gobbler hunting. Many state lands, particularly in Eastern and Osceola range, do not have the turkey densities found on adjacent private lands. And on the smaller tracts, you'll run into other callers in hot pursuit of pressured gobblers. But if you research well and pitch a camp in prime and remote turkey range, you can experience great hunting for as little as $100 a week.

Contact a regional or district office of the U.S. Forest Service or BLM for maps and other hunt-planning data. State fish and game departments can provide sportsmen's brochures and maps of wildlife management areas in turkey country.

The Fee-Hunting Option

The term "fee hunting" turns off many sportsmen, but it shouldn't. It is quite possible for non-resident turkey hunters to gain access to private lands in many states for reasonable daily or weekly fees.

On several trips to Texas, for example, where virtually all Rio Grandes are found behind locked gates, my partners and I paid ranchers $100 to $200 a day to turkey hunt. We split the access fees, making our hunts very cost-efficient. The landowners turned us loose on thousands of lightly hunted acres, where most mornings we heard 20 or more turkeys gobble. Bagging two long-bearded Rios apiece on each hunt was no problem.

Most ranches in Texas are locked up tight by white-tailed deer hunting outfitters and clubs each fall. But many landowners roll out the welcome mat to spring gobbler hunters, whose access fees provide an off-season windfall.

Fee hunting can also be a great option for hunting Merriam's on Western ranches. Limited opportunities exist in Eastern and Osceola country.

In addition to access, some Western ranchers offer room and board in bunkhouses for reasonable daily fees. Going cowboy-style is

Fee hunting a Texas ranch is an excellent way to bag your Rio Grande. You pay a landowner a reasonable daily or weekly fee, and he turns you loose on private ground teeming with longbeards. Many ranchers offer convenient and affordable bunkhouse accommodations.

a fun, convenient and affordable way to hunt strong populations of Rio Grandes or Merriam's.

Many local chambers of commerce in the West can provide lists of landowners who offer fee turkey hunts. And check out *Turkey & Turkey Hunting* and other outdoor magazines, in which landowners often advertise their rates and services.

Guided Turkey Hunts

For sportsmen on a budget, spending upwards of $1,000 for a guided, three-day spring gobbler hunt is not an option. Or is it?

In Alabama I once ran across a guy from New Mexico who had planned three do-it-yourself adventures on public land, but who had failed to bag his cherished Eastern gobbler. I got to thinking: That fellow could have booked into a Southern lodge, hunted thousands of acres of private ground, enjoyed excellent odds of bagging a long-bearded gobbler and saved money to boot.

If you're strapped for vacation time (who isn't these days?) and can scrape together the cash, consider a guided turkey hunt on occasion. Turkey hunting outfitters with access to huge tracts of private land abound across Eastern, Merriam's and Rio Grande range. Hiring an experienced guide who hunts the limited number of large ranches remaining in rural Florida is undoubtedly the best way to hunt the Osceola subspecies.

Many state fish and game agencies can provide lists of licensed hunting guides. Check a guide's references thoroughly before booking the turkey hunt of a lifetime. Outfitter rates vary widely, from several hundred dollars to more than $1,000 for a three-day spring gobbler hunt. Lodge accommodations range from Spartan to posh.

Do not feel that a guided hunt will somehow taint your quest for a grand slam. Each time I visit a lodge, I let my guide put me into prime turkey country, and then I do the maneuvering and calling. The good outfitters realize that serious turkey hunters seeking a slam must call their own gobblers.

I have been fortunate enough to hunt at many commercial turkey hunting

Don't feel your quest for a grand slam will be tainted if you visit a commercial lodge for an outfitted hunt. I let guides put me in gobbler hot spots, then do the maneuvering and calling myself.

lodges across the country in recent years. Here are a few that I recommend without reservation. All offer good meals, comfortable accommodations and friendly and experienced guides. Best of all, each operation hunts thousands of acres of well-managed ground teeming with longbeards. Hunter success rates are sky-high most springs.

For Easterns:

Bent Creek Lodge
PO Box 4267
Jachin, AL 36910
(205) 398-3130

White Oak Plantation
Route 1, Box 25
Tuskegee, AL 36083
(205) 727-9258

Tara Wildlife Services
6791 Eagle Lake Road
Vicksburg, MS 39180
(601) 279-4261

**Portland Landing
  Hunting Reserve**
3201 International Drive
Selma, AL 36701
(205) 875-2414

Turkey Trot Acres
Candor, NY 13743
(607) 659-7849

For Rio Grandes:

Twin Oaks Hunting Resort
PO Box 743
Woodsboro, TX 78393
(512) 543-4447

For Merriam's:

Vermejo Park Ranch
PO Drawer E
Raton, NM 87740
(505) 445-3097

For Osceolas:

Outdoor Adventures
Jim Conley
606 Pinar Drive
Orlando, FL 32825
(407) 249-1387

Travel Tips

Driving to faraway turkey country is most affordable and practical, particularly if you and a hunting buddy share the driving time and gasoline costs. Pack shotguns, duffels and camping gear into a vehicle, and away you go.

Motor along in a four-wheel-drive pickup or sport utility if at all possible. I once flew to Mississippi, rented a car and drove to a commercial lodge, where I hunted on my own for four days. Problem was, I couldn't negotiate the rain-slicked clay roads in my four-door sedan. I couldn't hunt where I needed to, and hence I failed to kill a gobbler.

If you fly on a super-saver ticket, which is most affordable when traveling thousands of miles to turkey hunt, call rental car agencies well in advance of your trip to reserve a 4x4 truck or sport utility. Most agencies offer a limited number of off-road vehicles, and they're expensive to lease. But most of the time, you will need one to get to the turkeys.

Contact local chambers of commerce and state wildlife agencies for lists of public and private campgrounds in potential gobbler zones. Camping is a budget-friendly and rewarding way to fill one or more legs of your turkey slam. Many ranchers in Rio Grande and Merriam's country will let you pitch a camp when you fee-hunt their lands.

Staying in an economy motel near your hunting area isn't as convenient as camping (you'll have to get up at 3:00 or 4:00 a.m. each morning and drive for miles to hunt gobblers leaving their roosts), but it's comfortable. A $40-a-day motel is more than affordable, particularly when you split the cost with a partner or two.

When planning your itinerary, try to hunt two subspecies of turkeys on a single trip. For instance, you might hunt Easterns in Missouri or Arkansas, then drive south to central Texas for Rios. Or you might duel Easterns in Alabama or Georgia and motor south to central Florida for a crack at an Osceola. The more gobblers you hunt on a circuit, the more affordable and exciting your quest for a grand slam becomes.

You'll have to head to the cypress swamps of central or southern Florida to duel an Osceola gobbler, typically the capstone of a hunter's grand slam. Going with a guide is the best way to hunt the Florida turkey in its restricted habitat.

In this vein, many sportsmen with unlimited time and money crisscross the country and complete their gobbler slams in a single spring season. But for most of us, a go-slow approach is more practical and affordable. I killed my first Eastern gobbler as a young boy in Virginia. Twenty years later, I capped my grand slam by shooting a sharp-spurred, 17-pound Osceola near Orlando.

Summary

Hone your hunting, maneuvering and calling skills on the race of wild turkey found near your home. As vacation time and funds allow, venture out to hunt another subspecies or two.

On each trip, spend a minimum of five to seven days in new turkey country. Don't shortchange your quest for a grand slam by limiting your scouting and hunting time.

Plan your hunts wisely over the years until you find yourself yelping in an intriguing piece of country far from home, staring down your shotgun barrel at that fourth coveted longbeard. Be still your racing heart! Place the gun's front bead on the base of the gobbler's neck, press the trigger and experience the zenith of spring turkey hunting.

My long-barreled Remington, woodland camo and wrinkle-free face date me here. Many years ago I hunted the "Wet Rat," aptly named for his matted feathers and scraggly beard. The old turkey became a symbol of the changing countryside in my native Virginia.

Chapter 17

Gobblers I Have Known

I paused in the logging road on the near side of the power line, not wanting to cross the opening in case the gobbler was roosted in the pines on the opposite edge. It was one of those damp, drizzly mornings in May when daylight comes late and covers your movements, but I was still leery of bumping the turkey. I sat on a wet log and listened as the foggy woodlot came to life.

Rain or shine, every spring morning is a new beginning, the first day of the rest of your life. As the black woods turn to silver and then to amber, you can sit listening for turkeys to gobble while contemplating all sorts of things going on in your life.

This dreary morning I pondered the fate of the James farm, a hallowed place where I had hunted white-tailed deer and wild turkeys for as many years as I could remember. When I began coming here with all the game-killing zest of a young teen, the farm was 200 acres in size, a perfect blend of fields and forest surrounded by large tracts of private land. It was a special and comfortable little place to kill a couple of bucks every autumn and a long-bearded turkey or two each spring.

But the past decade had brought a whirlwind of change to our small Virginia town. Commuters had flocked en masse from the big city to enjoy a taste of our country life. Suburbia had sprawled into our once quiet and slow-paced community. Subdivisions, shopping centers and a maze of new roads had been carved into the heart of our county.

For years the farm had sat a lame duck, the slitting edge of progress at its throat but dormant. Then seemingly overnight, a 20-house subdivision had popped up on the western edge of the property. Bulldozers ripped roads through the woods into the power line from all directions. The neighboring landowners were selling lots like hotcakes and making out like bandits. It was only a matter of time until old man James bit the bullet, sold his cattle and turned a small fortune by selling out to a big housing developer from the city.

I remember listening from this very spot a decade ago on those soft spring mornings. I would hear nothing but the sweet sounds of the rural South—cows mooing in the nearby pasture, whippoorwills and barrel owls ringing the misty woods with their melodies, songbirds flitting about and whistling gaily. Now dogs barked, house doors slammed and cars fired up all around as people zoomed away on their frenzied commutes into the city while I sat silently hoping for a turkey to gobble.

The population dynamics of our county were changing fast. I worried mostly about how this would affect the quality of my life. I also pondered the impact it would have on our resident game.

I wasn't too concerned about the whitetails. The adaptable deer would continue to thrive in the little woodlot, living right beside the city people, bedding close to their new homes and walking across their backyards at night, pausing to nibble their azaleas and fruit trees. But I was worried that all this human encroachment would push the flock of turkeys off the farm.

Gray half-light seeped into the woods. A house light flickered on through the hardwoods two ridges over. More vehicles fired up in driveways and roared out onto the county road. Then *gaaaarrr-roaabbble* from the pines across the power line. The "Wet Rat" was still there!

I had given the turkey his odd name the first time I had hunted him, on a damp, dank morning like this one a week ago. After slipping across the power line in the pitch-black darkness, I had set up against an enormous oak tree that had been on the farm since the days when our native sons, Stonewall Jackson and Colonel John Mosby, had chased the Yankees from this part of Virginia. The old oak sat atop a knoll where you could listen for a turkey to gobble while envisioning Civil War soldiers clashing fiercely for our soil in the foggy predawn. The oak tree was my favorite listening post for a variety of reasons.

With the woodlot swirling in heavy mist, the turkey had gobbled on his own—in a pine tree 50 yards from my setup! I flinched and peeked up and saw his odd silhouette etched against the pewter sky. The gobbler's feathers were soaked and matted after a long night of sleeping in the drizzling rain. This made his glimmering white head and neck look enormous, twice their normal size. The turkey's tail feathers were wet, dark and frazzled, and his long, scraggly beard was stuck together like a thin strand of licorice. "You look like a wet rat," I had whispered to the turkey before contemplating just what to do with him roosted so close to me.

If I moved to pull a call from my pocket, the turkey would surely bust me. My best bet would be to inch my shotgun barrel around toward his roost tree and then wait silently for the wet one to fly down. If he pitched out on my side, he would be in killing range. I could take him without uttering a call.

That would have been the smart thing to do. I could have bagged the gobbler, toted him back to town and shown him off outside the diner, treating my turkey hunting competition to a grand tale of how I deftly worked the old longbeard off his limb and into shooting range. But then I would only have been fooling myself. I would have missed the high-wire tension of luring the gobbler with simulated hen calls, the true essence of the spring obsession.

I had waited for the water-logged gobbler to turn on his limb, then eased a diaphragm call from my shirt pocket. Still, I had a big-time dilemma.

If I yelped so closely to the turkey, he would simply peek down and look for the hen. Seeing no feathers, he would be leery of flying down my way. But I had to try something. I eked out a soft tree yelp. *Gaaaarrrroaabbbble, gaaaarrrroaabbbble, gaaaarrrroaabbbble!* I jumped two feet in the air when the Wet Rat triple gobbled in my face, but somehow he hadn't seen me.

Trouble was, he hadn't seen the hen either. The turkey hung on his limb until 7:00 a.m. and gobbled more than 100 times.

As he roared, some odd thoughts struck me. Surely all the city folks leaving for work could hear his raucous melody. Then again maybe not—their ears were not tuned to calls of the wild. Could they envision a camouflaged country boy sitting in the damp, dreary woods, smiling and shivering to the bone every time the king of birds bellowed his love tunes? I doubt if those groggy-eyed people knew or gave a damn what was unfolding under their noses as they rushed off to manage another day in their hectic lives.

Suddenly the Rat sailed from his limb and glided away down the power line. I vowed to return to duel with him for the remainder of the season, even though I had much larger and better farms to hunt. The drenched turkey had somehow become a symbol of the changing times in my Virginia.

Hunting the gobbler six mornings in a row, I had patterned his movements. After flying from his pine roost, he would swing west, cut within 100 yards of a new house, cross a freshly dug dirt road into a vacant lot and strut back around toward the power line in search of hens.

On that seventh drizzly morning, I slipped back into the woods, made a huge circle, crossed the power line 400 yards below the Rat and slipped within 300 yards of his roost tree. There I set up. Normally I like to sneak much closer to a gobbling turkey, but I had already tried six tight positions on the Rat. He had no hens and gobbled his head off on the roost. But when his big feet touched the earth, he clammed up and began his strut circle, completely shunning my calling.

I admired that. The last gobbler to inhabit this dwindling little piece of southern wilderness, he was showing his fierce independence. And so doing, he was giving me the opportunity to hunt him every morning on the farm, something I would not be able to do in springs to come.

From my setup, I could barely hear the tom ringing the damp woods with his tree gobbles. When he clammed up, I knew he was on the ground and moving. I gave him 15 minutes to make his circle. During that time, houselights blinked on through the trees, more cars sped away, three dogs barked and someone took out their trash, capping the aluminum can with a booming clatter. When the woods quieted down a little bit, I yelped softly on a diaphragm.

Gaaaarrrroaabbbble! The turkey was right where I expected him to be, and this time I sensed he was coming.

I smiled when the Wet Rat popped up in the glistening green foliage. His white head glimmered like a softball above a bundle of slick onyx feathers. His scraggly beard was 10 inches long, but no thicker than a black crayon. When he exploded into strut, his rumpled tail feathers matted together, beautiful in an ugly sort of way. The Rat hadn't been dry for a week during the rainy spell, and he showed it.

Then my Remington boomed for the last time on the James farm.

As I slung the soggy gobbler over my shoulder, feeling his sharp spurs in my hand, an odd chorus of sounds greeted the sun, which finally popped from the gray clouds, bright and hot. Songbirds yodeled their beautiful melodies in the heat-rising mist. Crows cawed wildly. Cattle mooed in the pasture. Somewhere down the power line, a bulldozer fired up. Carpenters hammered away on another new home in the subdivision to the west. It seemed like a weird dream as I walked away from the farm a final time.

As we progress into the 21st century, spring gobbler hunting faces all sorts of challenges. The antics of the anti-hunters aside, no threat is greater than the loss of private farms and woodlots across the country, those hallowed little places where for decades boys have gone to turkey hunt and turn the corner to manhood. This saddens me, but there is nothing I can do about it. I just roll with the punches and smile every time I ride by what is left of the old James place, always remembering the Wet Rat.

My First Rio

My first encounter with the Rio Grande wild turkey occurred on a hot, sunny afternoon years ago near the little town of Comanche, Texas. A friend had arranged a couple of days of calling on a small ranch in the northern fringe of the Hill Country. I was as excited as a kid in a toy store as I set out across the sprawling grassland in search of a new breed of gobbler.

What strikes you first is how vast and rugged Rio Grande country appears. It is a dry, rough-cut land of bone-dry washes, gullies, ridges and plateaus carpeted with miles upon miles of thick mesquite and thorny cactus. Initially you will think it an odd place to find wild turkeys. But get to hunting around and it soon becomes evident that the moonscape is quite hospitable to your quarry.

The endless mesquite is actually a haven of turkey cover. Fields and grassland edges provide hundreds of varieties of flora and insects for hens to feast upon. Gobbler strutting grounds are unlimited. If you can find an alluvial creek bottom rimmed

It took all of 30 minutes to call in and shoot my first Rio Grande gobbler, which sported a 10-inch beard and weighed 26 pounds. I then left Texas with my second turkey tag unfilled. Like all races of wild turkeys, Rios will quickly humble over-confident hunters.

with cottonwoods or gnarled live oaks that Rios prefer for roosting, you will discover a surprisingly verdant turkey paradise in springtime.

Along a cool stream that snaked like an enormous rattler through the Hill Country ranch is where I thought I heard a Rio Grande tom

gobble for the first time. Prospecting through the sun-baked mesquite, breathing the sparkling April air and feeling wonderfully
alive and free, I paused to cutt on a slate call.

Obbblee.

What was that?

I cutt again.

Obbblee. It was definitely a gobble, though it sounded as if it had
come from a baby turkey.

Rio Grandes gobble freely in the spring, but their amorous calling to hens is neither as intense nor as rattling as that of Eastern
toms that roar deep in woodlands. There is no dialectical difference
between the two most abundant strains of gobblers in America. A
Rio simply sounds as if his head is stuck in a coffee can when he gobbles because of the acoustics of the open country he inhabits.

I drew a line on the muffled gobbling, slipped 50 yards through
the mesquite and yelped on a diaphragm call to simulate the sassy
calling of a hot little hen looking for some afternoon delight. Ready,
willing and able to accommodate every female turkey in Texas, a
huge gobbler flashed from a gully and strode toward me.

The Rio Grande is the heavyweight of the wild turkey clan!
Many biologists do not support my claim, but I believe you will the
first time you lay eyes on a dominant Texas tom. The 26-pound gobbler body-rocked to my calling on pink legs that looked like stilts. At
35 yards he pulled up to scan the mesquite for the calling hen, twisting his long crimson periscope and softball-size head in frantic circles. The lovesick turkey looked as big as an ostrich when I pressed
the Remington's trigger.

Ah, the big gobblers of the Southwest are shimmering objects of
beauty. The Rio Grande turkey's coloration is similar to the Eastern's, except that the Rio's rump coverts and tail-feather tips are a
lighter cinnamon-buff. Stroking my first Rio, I found his iridescence
striking. The afternoon sunlight spun a splendid spiderweb of gold,
purple, crimson and green on the turkey's ebony breast feathers.

I observed that the Rio's vivid pink legs are longer than the Eastern's, perhaps to better negotiate his rough-cut habitat. The spurs
on my first gobbler were over an inch long and sanded slightly at the
tips. The tom's 10-inch beard was thick and frazzled on the edges
from dragging the dry ground. When I lay the gobbler in a bed of sun-
drenched bluebonnets to spice my photographs with color, the Rio
radiated a rugged beauty I had never noticed in wild turkeys before.

It had taken all of 30 minutes to locate, yelp in and shoot my first
Rio Grande gobbler. Smiling all over myself, I decided to hunt selec-
tively for an even bigger Texas tom.

With the crimson sunrise blazing the eastern sky the next morning, I worked 20 turkeys in a creek bottom roost. I called in two crazy jakes, but six longbeards with hens thumbed their beaks at my finest yelping. I vowed revenge and struck out across the sun-glistening mesquite to hunt up a midmorning gobbler.

I find midday turkey hunting fascinating, especially in this broken country where you can twist and wind through pockets of mesquite and prickly pear, sneaking for miles if you want to. It is fast, fun, spontaneous calling. Time to coyote howl and crow call aggressively. Set up and hen cutt in loud, spirited series. Move again and pour the coals to your calling. Rios are like Easterns—they don't gobble all that much on their own up in the day. But if you persevere and sneak along and set up every couple of hundred yards or so, lonely gobblers will hammer your calling and break toward you with amazing regularity.

From a mesquite setup at high noon, I heard the tom's baby gobble and watched him come from 300 yards away, craning his red neck and twisting his crinkly white head to listen for the crazy-cutting hen. I really enjoy this aspect of hunting open-country birds. You can switch calls and tones and watch how a gobbler reacts. You can see him stop and extend his periscope and peer hard into the mesquite for you, or run straight toward a sweet- sounding call or ignore another one. This helps your calling immensely because you learn to understand the tendencies of an approaching gobbler.

This old tom liked the sound of my loud, raspy diaphragm calling, so I poured it to him. Though the turkey never gobbled again, he came steadily, strutting grandly in the sun and cutting the distance between us in 10 exhilarating minutes.

With the turkey at 40 yards I leveled the gun barrel on his crimson caruncles, sneered with delight for pulling him so far with such excellent calling and felt the shotgun's trigger.

Then I watched in amazement as the gobbler flinched, broke strut, putted and darted away across the grassland, acting if he had just seen a ghost. Actually he had, somehow picking my camouflage silhouette from the cover.

I left Texas later that day with one big gobbler packed on ice, one unfilled turkey tag and some interesting perspectives on traveling southwest to hunt the Rio Grande subspecies.

Foremost, Rios are unbelievably plentiful. I venture to say that if you hunt a prime Texas ranch during a peak gobbling phase in April, you will hear, see and work more gobblers in three days of hunting than you might in three or four seasons back home.

Secondly, calling in Rio country is a delight. If you have turkey hunted all your life in eastern hardwood forests or dense southern swamps, you will enjoy the miles of arid, mesquite-dotted grasslands, where you can hunt as far and as aggressively as you please all day and be assured of finding clear-throated gobblers to yelp to.

Finally, it is enjoyable to experience the traits of a new breed of gobbler. Tactically, hunting Easterns and Rios is pretty much the same, with habitat-induced idiosyncrasies of course. Like all wild gobblers, Rio Grandes are uncannily unpredictable—some are ridiculously easy to hunt, while others, especially those with hens, shun your calling like the worst Eastern toms.

If you are a skilled woodsman and caller, you will do well on these largely underhunted turkeys. But don't go West brimming with cockiness. Any notion that Rio Grandes are pushovers to hunt is nonsense. I can say from experience that long-bearded Rios can and will humble you quickly.

The Bull Turkey

I remember standing in a river bottom that sparkling May afternoon, craning my neck back to look high into the Sangre de Cristo Mountains, thinking, "What wild topography for wild turkeys!"

In the verdant valleys around 6,500 feet in elevation, where glittering streams coursed through greening parks and meadows rimmed with ponderosa pines and stands of pinyon and oak, you would expect to find hens and gobblers feeding, strutting, breeding and roosting in springtime. But what about those steep, rugged ridges and canyons at 10,000 feet, just below the glimmering snowline? Those would be prime haunts for elk and mule deer, but could America's only feathered big game live up there?

"Lots of turkeys in the high country," the ranch manager read my mind. Intrigued, I grabbed my turkey calls, hopped into a pickup and drove straight uphill over rocky, twisting roads for an hour in hopes of roosting a gobbler for the next morning's hunt.

I paused every 100 yards or so just below the snow to call down into steep-faced canyons and coulees. With minimal effort, I had 20 turkeys talking at dusk.

My how these Merriam's love to gobble! Going to roost, mature gobblers in peak breeding mode will hammer any type of turkey calling device. They respond well to owl, crow, coyote and other locator calls. Slam a truck door or toot a horn and a turkey will probably answer. The fact that you can shock so many gobbles out of these mountain dwellers adds zest to the hunting.

Chasing the beautiful Bull Turkey in the New Mexico high country reminded me of hunting bugling elk in autumn.

Set up on an 8,000-foot ridge the next morning, shivering in the sharp-edged air, I thought it would be fitting to bugle and chuckle like a bull elk on a diaphragm call. *Eaaaauuuueeeeee, ugg, ugg, ugg, ugg*. The gobbler must have forgotten that it was May and not September. He bellowed at my elk mating call and I immediately coined him the "Bull Turkey."

I slipped down a rocky ridge and set up on a bluff 100 yards above the gobbler. With pink glimmering on the vast horizon, I tree yelped on a raspy box. The turkey boomed a double gobble. I smiled coyly, confident the Bull was in the bag.

Remember what we said about getting cocky in Rio Grande country? The same applies when hunting the Merriam's subspecies. I listened as the Bull pitched down from his pine limb, gathered his hens and marched defiantly away from my yelping. Like a bad old Eastern would do, the bull tossed me a cursory gobble as he left the mountainside.

In addition to humbling cocky turkey hunters, Merriam's and Rios have another thing in common. Both strains of gobblers and hens are in a big hurry to get to prime feeding, strutting and breeding grounds once their big red feet hit the ground each morning. You must move with the vagabond turkeys, climbing ridges and hiking down canyons, shimmying over deadfalls in pine forests, sweating and breathing hard in the thin mountain air, pausing here and there to call and glass for game, forever circling around and trying to cut off a long-bearded gobbler as you would try to intercept a bull elk running with cows. Like elk hunting, the pursuit of Merriam's turkeys is physically demanding and emotionally invigorating.

I climbed and sweated in the New Mexico high country for two hours before I finally gained a vantage on the Bull Turkey. Actually, all that maneuvering worked to my advantage. By midmorning, the tom's hens had left for the nest. Sitting in the sparkling sunshine at 7,500 feet, I yelped on box call. The lonely Bull responded immediately.

I watched as the gobbler strutted 200 yards across an open park, thinking, "Is there a more beautiful wild turkey on earth than the Merriam's?" The tom's black feathers shone blue, bronze and purple in the sunlight. The long, silky tips of his fanned tail gleamed like polished ivory.

If you hunt with the right frame of mind, you will feel at once happy and sad when you align your shotgun barrel upon the crimson neck of such a striking quarry. I pressed the trigger and the load of No. 4 shot took the gobbler cleanly.

I admired the 19-pounder, by sheer weight an above average Merriam's. His blond-tipped tail coverts were impressive, as was his 10-inch beard. And so were his spurs in an odd sort of way. Not long, curved and sharp, but round and three quarters of an inch. The gobbler had lived four hard years in the rugged mountains, which had sanded the tips of his fighting spurs. I traced my fingers over the nubs, thinking they gave the Bull Turkey even more character.

The Swamp Ghost

I sat shivering in my palm-frond blind as the swamp came eerily to life. The towering cypress trees with their gaudy draperies of moss caught fire, engulfed in the crimson flame of dawn. Heavy mist swirled. Alligators splashed and birds shrieked, screamed and cawed. Amid it all, *obbllllee,* one short, muffled gobble. Then all was quiet again, except for the haunting sounds of the Florida backcountry at dawn.

"These Osceolas are mystery birds," Jim Conley whispered as we walked through a glistening oak hammock at 9:00 a.m. With the April sun racing high into the sky, our morning hunt was over. But my quest for an Osceola gobbler, the last link in my grand slam, was just beginning as Conley, one of the finest turkey guides in the Sunshine State, filled me in on the nuances of *Meleagris gallopavo osceola.*

The Osceola wild turkey is a ghost-like bird primarily because its range and population are limited. "The true Osceola is found from Jacksonville in the east to the mouth of the Suwannee River in the west, and south to the Everglades," Conley told me.

Owing to this restricted range, relatively few hunters pursue the Florida turkey each spring. Those who do hunt the land of sun and fun encounter a striking subspecies.

A streamlined version of the Eastern wild turkey, a hard-breeding Osceola gobbler may weigh a scant 16 pounds in April. In the bright Florida sunlight, the feathers on his back shimmer red, blue and green. Most distinctive are his wing primaries—black with narrow, irregular white veins. A mature Osceola's beard drags the ground, but is generally thinner than an Eastern tom's. The Florida turkey has long legs for walking in swamp water. His long, sharp spurs are coveted by hunters.

The Osceola is not only a beautiful wild turkey, he is an enigma. "These gobblers generally roost away from hens in cypress trees on the edge of big swamps," Conley said. "Back in there, their gobbling sounds muffled and farther away than it really is. Take that gobbler we heard this morning—he was roosted only 150 to 200 yards away."

To me, the ghost had sounded a mile distant.

"At first light, the turkeys sail out of the swamps and fly down into nearby pastures to feed and strut," Conley continued. "Then when the suns rises, burning the mist from the pastures and singeing the black feathers of the strutting gobblers, the birds retreat to the shade of swamps and oak hammocks and remain largely silent and inactive throughout the day."

Conley, a turkey hunting addict, scouts and photographs Osceolas year-round. This constant monitoring of the quarry has allowed my friend to tailor a simple but smart hunting strategy to the Osceola's spring behavior.

Having patterned turkeys using a stretch of pasture, Conley selects a calling site on the edge of an oak hammock. He cuts and weaves a palm-frond blind—nothing elaborate, simply a little hide to break his outline. On spring mornings, he sets a hen decoy 30 yards away, slips into his blind and tree clucks and yelps softly and sparingly as a nearby swamp comes to life.

The "Swamp Ghost" never gobbled the morning I bagged him. He just glided from a Florida cypress swamp and into my life on silent wings, capping my grand slam in mysterious fashion.

Conley's technique is successful because it is weaved around the most important tenet in spring turkey hunting. Having scouted and set up where turkeys feel comfortable gathering each morning, he has three-fourths of the battle won.

Having begun an hour earlier in the oak hammock near our blinds, my crash course in Osceola behavior was now complete as Conley pulled his Suburban alongside his mobile-home camp that sits in the shade of palm trees on a ranch outside of Orlando. After lunch, an afternoon nap in the air-conditioning and some bass fishing and gator watching that evening, we sat on the front porch of the trailer, sipping cold beer, swatting mosquitoes and planning the next dawn's duel.

"Let's go back to the same swamp," Conley offered. "I know turkeys are there."

"Fine with me," I responded, "I want a peek at that ghost."

I sat in my little blind at dawn, scanning the mist that danced on the pasture, listening intently. Crimson blazed the sky. Once again, the cypress swamp loomed before me like a haunted house on fire. The gators splashed and the birds screeched, but still no gobbling. I slipped a stacked-frame diaphragm into my mouth and tossed out a couple of raspy yelps.

Then I shivered and froze.

Forty yards away, an Osceola gobbler pirouetted around our decoy. Where had he come from, ghosting from the swamp and into my life on silent wings, refusing to gobble or even drum? Was he a mature gobbler or a jake? It was difficult to tell in the early-morning mist.

The gobbler was edgy, half-strutting while spinning to survey the pasture. He turned sideways, and his long beard curved from his breast like a hand sickle.

The old monarch spun away, and I inched the Mossberg's barrel through the palm fronds. I clucked, and when the gobbler curled his glimmering white head my way, I pressed the trigger.

The shot echoed through the swamp and the turkey fell. "My Osceola!" I cried, and then Conley and I shook hands violently. I lifted the dark-winged ghost high into the haze, admiring his 11-inch beard and sharp hooks. The crimson sky burned brighter, the shrieking of the swamp birds reached a fevered pitch. In the haunting Florida backcountry, my wild turkey grand slam was mysteriously complete.

You and I should greet every spring season with a renewed vow to hunt ethically and safely. It will do our grand quarry and sport a lot of good.

Chapter 18

The Spring Hunter's Code Of Conduct

One April morning in the rolling hardwoods of Virginia, I could hardly believe my good fortune. It was dark as an underground coal mine, a strong 45 minutes before fly-down time, yet a gobbler was booming love tunes a mile down a ridge that I knew like the back of my hand.

I sneaked off into the predawn to hunt the hottest-gobbling turkey I had encountered in years. If ever there was a "gimme bird" sans hens, and I can assure you there are very few of those out there, he was it.

With cloak of darkness covering my every move, I crept within 100 yards of the gobbler's roost and slipped against a hickory tree. Humming along to the turkey's raucous melody, I pleaded for dawn to arrive.

"I wish you would quiet down a little bit," I whispered to the gobbler. You see, a lonesome tom roaring on his limb can draw hens from every direction. More problematic, all that gobbling can pull every other turkey hunter in the county into your hunt zone. But I was hunting a private and tightly controlled lease of 3,000 acres that morning, so I had little worry of human competition. The thought faded as the turkey's gobbling intensified.

The bird drummed and gobbled hundreds of times before streaks of pink and blue etched the silver skyline. I could take no more, so I tree clucked on a diaphragm. The turkey triple gobbled!

I should have stopped calling right then and there, but a hot-gobbling turkey turns you aggressive, overly so on many occasions. I took a chance and cackled. The gobbler pumped his wings and pitched down early, sounding as if an elephant had fallen from the sky. I pointed my shotgun and felt the safety as the white-headed bird body rocked into view.

Then a shotgun blast shattered the morning stillness. Did my gun malfunction and go off on its own? That was what struck me first. But then I heard the chilling sound of lead pellets ripping tree bark and mangling leaves beside me.

I flattened out and curled around the tree, recoiling in terror. I remember thinking about my wife and two young sons asleep back at the house as I ran my hands over my face and body. No pain, but I felt certain that I would feel my hot, running blood.

The poacher slid from the morning shadows with his shotgun poised for a follow-up shot. He searched wildly for the crippled gobbler, but the turkey had flopped away. Then he peered quizzically at me. I mustered the strength to whisper, "Don't shoot again."

Realizing his mistake, the poacher fled for the lease boundary, never to be seen again. To this day, I wonder how he feels about leaving a man possibly to die in the woods. How does he live with the thought of someone's blood on his hands?

Amazingly, I was unscathed. I stood weak-kneed in the peaceful and glistening woods, thoughts convulsing between disbelief and anger. Recreating the near tragedy, I determined that while I was calling the gobbler, the poacher was crawling in to bushwhack him. At 50 yards, the outlaw had knelt and fired at the turkey working to my calls. By the grace of God, I had been positioned 15 feet outside his line of fire.

What Price Turkey Hunting?

Is spring gobbler hunting an inherently dangerous sport? Has it simply outgrown itself? Is there anyplace, anytime, a hunter can go to experience the exhilaration and challenge of calling a wild turkey without looking over his shoulder and risking life or limb?

Such questions have haunted me since that fateful April morning years ago. And after much pondering, I have found the answers to be very complex.

Spring gobbler hunting is an intoxicating affair, with camouflaged hunters maneuvering like ghosts and hiding in the greening woods, calling to skittish turkeys whose gobbles seem to penetrate to the core of a man's soul. The sport's high-wire tension can cause people to lose their heads and react carelessly with firearms in their hands.

I do not believe turkey hunting is intrinsically hazardous. Many shooting-sports studies support my premise, stating that you are more apt to drown in a bathtub than to be injured in a hunting accident. Still, the potential for conflict is out there.

No and yes. That is how I respond to the question as to whether or not spring gobbler hunting has become too popular.

Wild turkey populations are at record levels across the country and should continue to increase steadily in the future. This creates unlimited potential for a burgeoning number of spring turkey hunters. But at the same time, access to private hunting lands, especially in the East, South and Midwest where most turkeys roam, is dwindling. There is increased competition on private tracts that remain open to sportsmen. And more and more turkey hunters are flocking to national forests, state wildlife areas and other public lands. This increased ratio of hunters per square mile of accessible turf is cause for concern.

Add to this the evils of poaching. My close call occurred on a tightly posted private lease that the landowner routinely patrols. Calling across America each spring, I hear of increasing amounts of unethical and illegal activity. Which means that each time you step out of your truck, you must remember that crime in the turkey woods can strike anywhere, anytime. A sad scenario, but that is just the way it is.

The ultimate question becomes: How does all this affect the future of spring turkey hunting? You may not want to hear this, but I believe the sport may become forever tainted unless every turkey hunter in America immediately begins to reassess his or her personal conviction to ethics and safety.

Ethical Turkey Hunting

Look deep into the window of your soul. Are you really a moral turkey hunter? Do you hunt only where you have permission, or do you slip across the fence on occasion if you hear a turkey gobbling on a neighboring piece of private property?

Do you give other hunters plenty of elbow room? Or do you sneak in on toms they are working, trying to shoot birds out from under your competition?

Do you respect America's grandest game bird, realizing that just working an old gobbler ringing the spring woods with nature's ultimate mating call is ample reward for any man? Do you call your toms well within shotgun or bow range and take only clean-killing shots? Or will you resort to bushwhacking a bad bird? Ever commit the ultimate atrocity of roost-shooting a gobbler? Do you possess that "kill a turkey at all costs" mentality that some hunters display in the sport?

I like to lay back in the glorious spring woods with every old gobbler that treats me to a thrilling battle. It is a relaxing and fulfilling way to show respect to my magnificent quarry.

Whether or not we care to admit it, each of us can find flaws in his turkey hunting philosophy. We would do the sport and the wild turkey a lot of good to greet this and every subsequent spring season with a new set of morals.

First, if you hunt on private land, always obtain written permission and stay within the boundaries. Know exactly how many other hunters are accessing the property, and exactly who they are. Respect the rights of legitimate hunters and demand the same in return.

I hope you never encounter a poacher, for I can assure you that the sound of lead pellets ripping bark and raking leaves beside you will taint your turkey hunting forever. But if you run across an outlaw or suspect illegal activity in your area, do not take the matter into your own hands. Contact the landowner and a local conservation officer. Turn poachers in and help to convict them, because they are not only stealing turkeys, but quite possibly jeopardizing your life.

Whether you hunt private or public lands, use your instincts and common sense. If there is a truck parked near a gobbling turkey, you can be reasonably sure another hunter is working him. This is not always the case. A hunter could have hiked three miles back into the woods before a tom cranked up next to his parking place. Still, common sense says to leave this situation alone. Come back another morning to see if the turkey is gobbling near the road again.

When approaching a gobbling bird, pause a minute to look and listen. Feel the vibes of the situation. Is that a hunter or a real hen calling to the gobbler? Generally, hunters in this day and age call much louder and more frequently than live hens do, though this is no surefire indicator. If there is the slightest doubt in your mind that another hunter might be in the area, leave. Walking away from a hot-gobbling turkey is tough, but it is the ethical and safe thing to do.

I believe that to kill many gobblers, you must maneuver on them. But never try to stalk or belly-crawl within shotgun range of a gobbling bird. In addition to being incredibly immoral, bushwhacking invites disaster if another hunter happens upon the scene. Besides, stalking turkeys is illegal in many states, as it should be.

Finally, it goes without saying that you must hunt within the bag limits of state law. Sadly, turkey hunting has become a numbers game in many circles—people believe they have to shoot one more gobbler than the next guy to become the local hero.

By all means, try to fill your turkey tags each spring. I sure do. But even if you come up a gobbler or two short, that is all right. Turkey hunting, if you are going about it correctly, is more about reveling in the pursuit of the grand quarry than killing. To shoot over your limit is one of the best ways I know to help destroy the sport.

Be Safe

Hunting ethically and safely go hand in glove. By avoiding potential conflicts with other hunters and poachers, you minimize the chance of disaster striking. Still, there are other critical safety precautions to bear in mind:

• Practice safe firearms handling at all times. Point your shotgun's muzzle safely toward the ground when loading shells. Unload your shotgun—both chamber and magazine—upon returning to vehicle, camp or home.

• Use your head and never wear red, white, blue or black socks, T-shirts or other clothing beneath your camouflage. If these colors somehow stick out (i.e. you set up to call and your camo pants ride up to reveal white and red-topped socks) a careless shooter may mistake you for a gobbler.

Setting up against wide-trunked trees, wearing complete camouflage and using common sense to avoid potential conflicts are good safety precautions for the spring woods.

- I like to use gobbler calls and decoys on occasion, but never on moderately to heavily hunted private or public lands. Gobble calls, fake turkeys and a lot of hunters slipping around the spring woods is an unsafe mix.
- Try to set up in fairly open areas where you can see 50 to 60 yards in as many directions as possible. Back up against a tree or fallen log as wide as your torso and as high as your head. If you see another hunter approaching your calling station, don't get up or wave your hands—sudden moves could be mistakenly viewed as a turkey flashing in the foliage. Whistle or speak out in a normal voice to alert another hunter of your presence.
- Before slipping off your shotgun's safety, positively identify a mature gobbler— look for his red, white or pale-blue head, dangling beard and evenly fanned tail feathers when he struts. Never take this seemingly simple task lightly. Statistics show that many accidents involving people mistaken for gobblers are initiated by experienced turkey hunters. A man weighing 180 pounds should never be mistaken for an 18-pound bird, but it happens every spring. Know your target!

Kids: The Future Of Spring Gobbler Hunting

Ethics and safety are cornerstones that will help our sport survive and flourish into the 21st century and beyond. But to my mind, all of that will be for naught unless we train new generations of responsible turkey hunters.

This spring, make it high priority to spend some quality time afield with your son, daughter, niece, nephew, grandchild or any other kid who is close to your heart. Calling in and shooting a sharp-spurred gobbler with a rope that drags the ground might seem to be the ultimate experience. But in reality, introducing children to the myriad wonders of the outdoors is a turkey hunting's top honor.

Take a child with you as you scout for gobblers. Point out tracks, droppings and scratchings in the leaves. Finding drag marks where strutting gobblers have gouged dirt roads or sandy creek bottoms with their heavy wings will excite both you and your son or daughter.

Before the season, hit the woods at dawn and dusk to locate roosted birds. Cut loose on an owl or crow call, and watch your child's eyes sparkle as he or she revels in the wild turkey's gobbling, one of nature's wildest and most thrilling sounds.

As you hike around the spring woods, encourage a youngster to find deer tracks and last fall's rubs and scrapes. Point to a red-tailed hawk in the sky. Tune a kid into the barking of a gray squirrel or the hammering of a pileated woodpecker. The outdoors is a new puzzle for young minds, which are hungry to discover all the pieces and fit them together.

In short, teach a child to enjoy and respect all that the Great Creator has given us. And when your kid grows to hunting age, it's time to get him or her that first gobbler.

In some states, a child must turn 12 before obtaining a turkey hunting license. But there is no age limit for learning to shoot a firearm. I encourage you to put a BB gun in your child's little hands as soon as you feel he or she is ready. Supervise kids closely at all times and forever preach firearms safety.

Some of my fondest memories are tagging along in the woods with my father. At six I was deciphering turkey and deer sign. By eight I was a crack shot with my BB gun. I was 10 years old when I began toting a shotgun under Will Hanback's intense supervision. We didn't have many gobblers in Virginia back then, but that was okay. I was enjoying the woods with my father, and that is all that really mattered.

When the time is right, enroll your youngster in a hunter safety course. Purchase him or her a 20-gauge shotgun (you can trim the stock to fit a child, or buy a youth model) and pattern it with 2 3/4-inch 4s or 6s. If you call a gobbler within 20 yards or so, your child can roll him cleanly.

Locate a gobbling turkey and set up to call with your camo kid tucked tightly inside your knees. Help him or her align the shotgun

Teaching kids close to our hearts to turkey hunt responsibly and safely will keep the spring sport in good hands for years to come. (Photo courtesy Mossy Oak)

barrel on the bird's flaming red neck at 20 paces. Shiver as one with your flesh and blood and whisper, "Take him."

Your child will be happy but probably speechless and you will be a kid at heart again when the two of you race out to claim your prize. Give your new hunting partner a big bear hug. Then sit awhile in the sunlit woods, smoothing the turkey's iridescent feathers and examining its beard and spurs. Be proud of your son or daughter and proud of yourself. You have done your part to ensure that the future of spring gobbler hunting is in good hands.

Appendix

For more information on the turkey hunting products recommended in this book, contact the following companies:

Realtree Camouflage
1390 Box Circle
Columbus, GA 31907
(706) 569-9101

Trebark Camouflage
3434 Buck Mt. Rd.
Roanoke, VA 24014
(703) 774-9248

Perfection Turkey Calls
P.O. Box 164
Stephenson, VA 22656
(703) 667-4608

Quaker Boy, Inc.
5455 Webster Road
Orchard Park, NY 14127
(716) 662-3979

Remington Arms Co.
1011 Centre Rd.
Delle Donne Corporate Center
Wilmington, DE 19805
(302) 993-8547

Mossberg, Inc.
7 Grasso Ave.
North Haven, CT 06473
(203) 230-5300

Mossy Oak Camouflage
P.O. Box 757
West Point, MS 39773
(800) 331-5624

Primos, Inc.
P.O. Box 12785
Jackson, MS 39236
(601) 366-1288

Knight & Hale Game Calls
Drawer 670

Cadiz, KY 42211
(502) 924-1755

M.A.D. Calls
1595 County Road, #256
Columbia, MO 65201
(314) 474-4516

Federal Cartridge Co.
900 Ehlen Drive
Anoka, MN 55303
(612) 323-2300

Feather Flex Decoys
1655 Swan Lake Rd.
Bossier City, LA 71111
(318) 746-8596

Higdon Motion Decoy, Inc.
#7 Universal Way
Metropolis, IL 62960
(618) 524-3385

Winchester Ammunition
427 North Shamrock
East Alton, IL 62024
(618) 258-2000

W. C. Russell Moccasin Co.
260 S.W. Franklin St.
Berlin, WI 59423
(414) 361-2252

Precision Shooting Equipment
2727 North Fairview
Tucson, AZ 85703
(602) 884-9065

Golden Eagle Archery
1111 Corporate Drive
Farmington, NY 14425
(716) 924-1880

Index

256